The Proper Care of
CANARIES

TW-114

Opposite: *This pair of Border canaries represents what most people believe to be "typical" of the species. There are, however, many other varieties and colors that have become highly popular.*

Photography and illustrations:
Dr. Herbert R. Axelrod, David Alderton, H.Bielfeld, Michael DeFreitas, P. Demko, Isabelle Francais, Michael Gilroy, Harry V. Lacey, Horst Mayer, Ron & Val Moat, H. Mueller, Robert Pearcy, Donald Perez, John Quinn, Mervin F. Roberts, Vogelpark Walsrode.

Distributed in the UNITED STATES to the Pet Trade by T.F.H. Publications, Inc., One T.F.H. Plaza, Neptune City, NJ 07753; distributed in the UNITED STATES to the Bookstore and Library Trade by National Book Network, Inc. 4720 Boston Way, Lanham MD 20706; in CANADA to the Pet Trade by H & L Pet Supplies Inc., 27 Kingston Crescent, Kitchener, Ontario N2B 2T6; Rolf C. Hagen Ltd., 3225 Sartelon Street, Montreal 382 Quebec; in CANADA to the Book Trade by Macmillan of Canada (A Division of Canada Publishing Corporation), 164 Commander Boulevard, Agincourt, Ontario M1S 3C7; in ENGLAND by T.F.H. Publications, PO Box 15, Waterlooville PO7 6BQ; in AUSTRALIA AND THE SOUTH PACIFIC by T.F.H. (Australia), Pty. Ltd., Box 149, Brookvale 2100 N.S.W., Australia; in NEW ZEALAND by Brooklands Aquarium Ltd., 5 McGiven Drive, New Plymouth, RD1 New Zealand; in the PHILIPPINES by Bio-Research, 5 Lippay Street, San Lorenzo Village, Makati, Rizal; in SOUTH AFRICA by Multipet Pty. Ltd., P.O. Box 35347, Northway, 4065, South Africa. Published by T.F.H. Publications, Inc. Manufactured in the United States of America by T.F.H. Publications, Inc.

The Proper Care of
CANARIES

John Porter

This variegated intensive red canary is just one of the many color mutations that developed from the original "wild" canary.

Contents

The European Goldtinch is one of the species belonging to the sub-order of birds called Oscines—the canary is another member.

Introduction

As an ornamental resident of a cage or aviary, the canary has undoubtedly been kept in greater numbers than any other bird species. For about four and a half centuries it was the world's most popular pet bird. Not until the 1950s did the budgerigar take over its crown as the king of caged birds. Today, this most attractive and talented songster is still very popular, and in recent years there has been somewhat of a revival of interest in

This Border canary is colored similarly to the original wild canary. The domestication of this beautiful songster opened the door to the world of birdkeeping.

both the well known varieties, and in many of the lesser seen breeds.

HISTORY OF THE CANARY

The origins of the domestic canary can be traced back to the wild canary (*Serinus canaria*). It is native to the islands of Azores, Maderia, and the Canary Islands for which it is named. These are located in the Atlantic Ocean and were possessions of Portugal until seized by Philip II of Spain in 1580. While the Portuguese no doubt captured and sold many of the little singing finches found on these islands, it is the Spanish who are historically credited with domesticating the canary and exporting it throughout their empire, as well as to most nearby countries in Europe.

The British, the French, and the Dutch breeders took over what the Spanish had started, and developed distinct varieties; both in physical appearance and color. Many old canary varieties have since become extinct, but before this happened others were created from them. Today you could choose from about 27 or so differing types, most of which are quite rare.

The popular varieties, seen in pet shops and at

The red-factor is a color variety which came about from crossing the canary with the Red-Hooded Siskin. This coloration cannot exist in birds that do not carry the red gene.

exhibitions, are nearly all of British origin that were developed during the early 1800s. England's singular advantage, regarding its animal breeding programs, was that its land was never ravaged by a succession of

There are several varieties of crested canaries, all of which are "type" varieties. A "type" canary is one which is bred for a particular character, shape, or feathering.

wars, (as was most of mainland Europe). It represented the one stable nation for many centuries, so breeding stocks were never decimated by invasions. This allowed type breeding to develop as an unbroken continuum. The subsequent growth of England's enormous empire enabled it to export its canary varieties around the world. This is why the most popular varieties nearly all carry names derived from the areas in Great Britain where they were developed.

WHAT IS A CANARY?

The canary is a member of the group of birds known as finches (family Fringillidae). This family is one of many found in the order known as Passeriformes—the perching birds. All of these birds have four toes, one of which is directed backwards and works in opposition to the three forward facing toes. This arrangement allows the birds to grasp branches without any effort. This is because the muscles in their "rest" position are closed, and the bird has to physically flex its muscles in order to release its hold of the branch, or whatever it is clinging to.

The chicks of passerine birds all have a unique gape by which they elicit food from their parents. The inside of their mouths are often variably colored with the beak edge being yellow, so as to be easily seen by the adults. Canaries are also members of the sub-order of birds called Oscines—the songbirds. In these birds, there are special throat muscles which enable them to produce a melodious song. Songs are variable and may simply be little "tweets," or truly magnificent. The canary's closest relatives are the serins, siskins, and such species as goldfinches and greenfinches.

Canaries are known in birdkeeping terms as "hardbills." This means they are able to break open the shells of seeds with their beaks. It is of course a rather loose term because many other birds can as easily crack the husks of seeds, the parrot-like birds especially so.

SINGING CANARIES

The male birds of all canary varieties are excellent songsters, and certain of them have been selectively bred to be especially melodious. These varieties are the Roller, the American Singer, the Timbrados, the Columbus, the Waterslager, and a few others. In these birds, type is not the major essential; the song is the important factor. The birds are carefully trained in order to achieve the excellence seen in the top class exhibition bird.

THE APPEAL OF CANARIES

The appeal of canaries stems from their many attributes. They are hardy finches, and have proven to be reliable and prolific breeders. They are colorful, being available in white, yellow, brown, green, rose, silver, and countless other shades and combinations of these. This makes them

The canary is one of the most popular household pets. It is a magnificent songster, has a beautiful appearance, and, (for those who wish to breed) it is very prolific.

great birds for those who like the challenge of color breeding.

They have endearing personalities, which makes them super pets, yet are glamorous and ideal birds for the potential exhibitor. They make excellent additions to a garden aviary, where their song and color is sure to make them favored residents. They do not, of course, destroy vegetation in the form of planted shrubs (as do the parrot-like birds), and they can be very long-lived for such relatively small birds. An average life-span would be in the order of ten years, however, it is not unknown for individuals to reach twice this age. Given all of these advantages it is not surprising that they have remained such popular birds for so many years.

Whether you simply plan to keep a single canary as a pet, or become a breeder and exhibitor, this book will give you all of the essential information needed to provide your canaries with the proper care they need. All aspects from stock and housing selection to breeding and health care are detailed. The text is illustrated throughout with gorgeous color photographs in order to provide you with both a written and a visual source of reference on these truly delightful birds.

Gold agate canary. The canary has proven to have a great capacity to produce mutations. Breeders experiment with these mutations and produce new variations from them.

Above: The birdroom has become popular among breeders who keep a number of canaries. It allows the breeder to have all of his stock within one location. **Opposite:** Sliding partitions can transform a cage from a single breeder to a double, and even to a triple. This is advantageous because it allows a pair of birds more space without moving them to a different location.

BIRDROOMS CAGES & AVIARIES

GENERAL CONSIDERATIONS

The type of accommodation you will choose for your canary(ies) will be governed by three basic factors. The first is how many birds you plan to keep, the second is how much space you have available, and the third is the amount of cash you are willing to invest

into housing the stock. If you intend to keep more than one or two pet birds, then your thoughts will be directed towards a birdroom, or one or more aviaries, or both. Exhibition canary breeders traditionally conduct their operations from birdrooms, and cages within these. However, aviary flights are strongly advised if you wish to retain vigor within your stock. This fact is often overlooked. If your plans are simply to breed nice canaries, this can be achieved either by cages, colony breeding, or by giving pairs their own external flight which leads to a large internal cage or small flight.

You may wonder why the exhibition breeder favors cage over aviary breeding. This is due to in a number of factors. Cage breeding is far less costly. Within the confines of a birdroom of only modest dimensions it is possible to house quite a lot of pairs. The cost of giving each of these pairs their own aviary would of course be beyond the available cash of the average breeder—who in any case may simply not have the space to erect the number of aviaries needed. Birdroom breeding thus allows the breeder to produce far more chicks per season than would otherwise be the case. Such numbers are

The mister is a great device in the birdroom. It will raise production if your chicks have trouble getting out of their shells. The water temperature should be near 32° C (90° F). If you plan to mist directly on the eggs, mist only; do not spray.

required in order to select the few quality birds that will be suitable for exhibition.

In a cage breeding system you are able to cater for more birds than would be possible with a large number of aviaries, in terms of the time factor needed. You are also able to control such matters as heat and light duration, which is not the case with an aviary breeding project. Finally, you have more control over the growth of the chicks because they can be monitored and helped more readily than in aviary situations. The exhibition bird must be trained from an early age, and again, its retention within a confined space is favored. As you can see, the advantages of cage breeding in birdrooms is related to numbers, time, training and cost—all practical considerations.

The main advantage of aviary breeding (even if the actual nests are in an attached birdroom), is that the chicks are invariably stronger and more fit. This is because they not only contend with more variable weather, thus temperatures, but also because they receive more exercise and benefit from the rays of the sun and rain. The weakest of aviary bred birds will not survive, whereas such birds in a cage may do well because of the protected environment in which they live. Such birds may have quality color and appearance, but not a lot of breeding vigor. The disadvantage of colony breeding is that you are not able to select which birds mate with which. This is an important factor in a domesticated species, such as the canary, where some control over the colors and potential quality of the stock is desirable. Your first thoughts should therefore be directed toward the reasons you wish to breed canaries, so that the accommodation can be prepared with this in mind.

Probably the best set up is a large birdroom to which a number of aviaries are attached.

Within the birdroom you can house many pairs of breeding birds, yet still allow them some aviary time on a rotational basis in order to exercise. If you do not have the space for either a birdroom or an aviary, you may still be able to house a number of breeding pairs if you have a spare room in your home.

SENSIBLE PLANNING

The majority of breeders are dissatisfied with their birds' accommodation by the time they gain one year or more of experience. Over this period they come to realize the failings of their original structures or layout. This is unavoidable to a certain degree, but you can, through sensible planning, limit the extent of likely dissatisfaction. For example, there are numerous ways in which cages can be constructed. If you commit totally to any one of these, you have little choice but to undertake time consuming and costly changes at a later date if they prove unsuited to your needs. Likewise, if you select a poor site for erecting a birdroom

An outdoor aviary flight may require to have a "false" roof added to it to help keep predators out. Mesh of this size is suitable for such a feature.

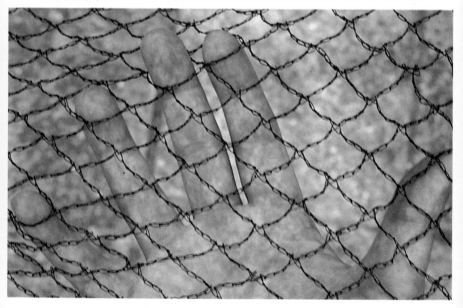

or aviary structure, you may regret this a year or so down the line when it proves too small because there is no room for extensions (assuming other sites were originally available).

You may have conversely chosen a fine site but ignored supplying the birdroom with such services as electricity, sewage, and water. If cost is a deterrant in supplying such facilities, what might be possible is to channel wiring into the structure so it could be connected to the mains at a future date. Likewise, piping for water and sewage could be incorporated into the original plans, even if it is not possible to hook

them into the mains at the time. This would save on having to rearrange the birdroom at a later date, but will enable you to feature these valuable additions.

It is also very prudent to use only quality materials when constructing anything to do with birds. This means the birdroom structure itself, the cages, the aviary covering (mesh), and all fittings within the birdroom. By doing so you will not have to virtually strip everything down in order to make it draftproof, or have to rehouse your stock while you repair or replace inexpensive aviary mesh or other

Breeding can take place within an outdoor flight. Plenty of light should be provided to breeding pairs. It is also a good idea to provide some type of heating system as well as a ventilation system.

supports because the first major high winds almost leveled your initial structure! Never rush into erecting a birdroom or aviary. Visit a number of breeders and see their set up. They will be happy to discuss with you the things they wish they had incorporated—as well as the features that have proved successful to their needs. Make notes, and from these you will be far less likely to make mistakes than if you just go ahead and build based on your own ideas. To proceed in haste and repent at leisure is most definitely true when applied to any aspect of animal husbandry. Within your initial planning, the one thing you can almost guarantee is that you will underestimate the space you will need if your interest in keeping canaries grows. With this in mind, always allow for expansion in your plans even if you do not commit to actual structures initially—which is also a wise thing not to do. Very often a person commences on a wave of enthusiasm only to lose interest later. Accept this possibility and proceed with it in mind.

THE BIRDROOM

The essentials of a good birdroom are that it give ample light and be draft resistant and damp free. It should also be as rodent proof as possible. If you live in a country, such as the USA or Australia, where snakes might be a problem, some consideration of their entry prevention would be wise. However, in the author's experience, if mice and rats cannot gain entry, neither will snakes, because mice and rats are usually more industrious. When snakes do gain entry it is usually via holes made by the rodents, by too large an aviary mesh size, or because an entrance door or a window to the birdroom, that is not protected by mesh, has been left open.

The choice of materials for the birdroom structure is usually between brick, in its various forms, or wood. In either case it is certainly very wise to line this with a suitable board and fill the cavity with good insulating material. This will greatly reduce your heating and cooling bills. If wood is used, give exterior walls a generous coating of preservative—and periodically treat it. By so doing, its life will be almost unlimited. The roof should be well covered with a waterproof felt or similar material. An overhang of the roof will give the walls some protection. Fit gutters so that rain is carried away.

A dark birdroom should be avoided, so ensure that there are ample windows. Alternatively, skylights will permit you to have maximum wall space for cages. Those of the opening type, will be more practical on very hot days. All windows and skylights should be covered with a fine weld-wire of about ½ in. (1.25 cm.) square. If you live in a hot country where insects are a problem, fine

An overhang of the roof on an outdoor aviary will channel the rain water away from the inside of the flight. This is a nice feature because it does not allow the aviary floor to become saturated, thus a messy place to work in and a health hazard for the birds.

mesh would of course be better.

The floor of the birdroom can be of concrete or wood. Either should be covered with suitable tiles or linoleum so that it can be cleaned very easily. If a wooden birdroom is erected, have it placed on bricks to a height of at least 6 in. (15 cm.). This will

A neat and uniform arrangement of cages, most of which have three compartments. The center compartment is slightly smaller which becomes useful when pairing one male to more than one female.

allow air to circulate underneath and will also deny rodents a place to hide. Regarding air circulation; the fitting of air vents is very much recommended. Place one (or more depending on the size of the birdroom) just above floor level and another just below ceiling level in the opposite corner of the room. Cover these with wire mesh if the openings would allow rodents or snakes to enter.

It is also worthwhile to build a safety porch in front of the entrance to the birdroom. This removes the risk of birds flying past you and away in the event they had somehow escaped their cage or indoor flight. The porch need only be a simple one of weld wire stapled to a suitable framework. Fit it, and the entrance door to the birdroom, with a good padlock—unfortunately bird thieves are on the increase.

The actual size of the birdroom is obviously dependent on available cash, space, likely stocking rate, and so on. In general, make it as spacious as possible and allow yourself ample room to stock seed, spare cages, and all of the other items you will quickly gather as your hobby develops. Rather than making the cages and working areas fit into the space available in a given birdroom, a better approach is to design the birdroom from the inside. Design the internal layout, allowing for the size and runs of cages you want, plus working surfaces, sink, storage cupboards, and the like. Next, allow a generous area, or walkway, for you to move around in, then see what size structure you will need.

Design the birdroom with some space allocation for future expansion. Apart from inside space, this also means allowing for a possible extension to the building itself. With this in mind, a second door could be incorporated at the other end of the room. If you extend, you will then not have to cut out a section of the wall, and have its attendant disturbance to the birds. On a cautionary note, if your initial birdroom is large and you still need more space later on, it might

be prudent to erect a second birdroom. This limits the risk of an epidemic wiping out all of your stock. The second birdroom should be located as far away as feasible from the first one. Only you can determine how many birds you feel should be kept in a given single space, but never risk overcrowding. This does not simply mean birds per cage, but also birds per given building or room.

The birdroom site should be protected, if possible, from adverse weather. This can be done via a wall, a row of shrubs, or by a fence erected as a windbreak. Avoid placing a birdroom or aviary directly under trees as

A single breeding pair of birds will appear to show a great deal of affection toward one another. The male will attempt to feed the hen, and will sing to her awaiting an invitation to mate.

these present many problems; falling leaves, dampness and fungi, wild bird droppings, insects in the summer, and so on. These all create either more work for you or increased health hazards for the birds.

CAGES

Your choice of cages is considerably greater today than in past years. The materials used can be metal, wood, plastic, or a combination of these. Opinions differ greatly on which are best, so we will look at each type.

For a single breeding pair of birds the very minimum cage size should be 12x12x12 in. (31x31x31 cm.). This is very small and a greater length and height is advisable. Wood is still the favored material for most enthusiasts, though the all metal cages are gaining in popularity. Wood is advantageous because

This is a typical show cage that can also be used as a stock cage within a birdroom. It consists of wood with a wire front.

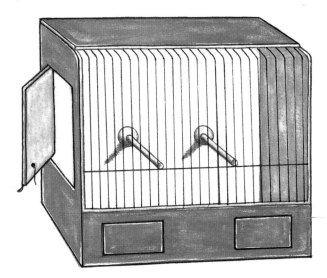

is easier for the handyperson to work with, and most commercially made breeder/stock cages are produced using this. The cages can be single, double, or continuous run units.

A double breeder cage means one which is twice as long as a single, and has a removable sliding partition. This enables the cage to be used as two small cages or one longer one. In the past the partitions were made of wood, but today they are usually clear Plexiglas or metal bars. The triple breeder is longer yet and has two slides.

A continuous run cage is simply a single, very long cage which has numerous sliding partitions; it can also be one structure in which there is a run of single, double, or various sized cages, but does not have partitions.

You might also build a run of cages that utilize the back and end walls of a birdroom, thus reducing the overall cost. You might have two, three, or four tiers of cages which are built in blocks, or you might have continuous run cages which are freestanding on a framework—called staging. Each of these systems has its advantages and drawbacks, so I would suggest you ponder them carefully. It may be best not to commit totally to one system until you have gained enough experience to determine which best suits your needs.

The main disadvantage of built-in

Hagen Products manufactures a variety of cages that a pet canary will thrive in. Your local pet shop dealer will be able to show you all the different varieties that are available.

cages is that you cannot rearrange your layout. Large blocks of cages are rather difficult to move around, but individual cages are more costly and never quite as neat and tidy. Initially, however, they are probably the best option until you get a few double and triple breeders. Later on, when you design the birdroom to meet your needs, these "loose" cages will come in handy as transport units, or spares that can be placed elsewhere if the need arises. If you purchase or build blocks of cages, fit them with castors (wheels) so you can move them around in order to thoroughly clean the floor and walls they butt up against.

An advantage of the modern, all metal cages is that they are hygienic. They provide few crevices for lice and other parasites to live and breed in. Further, the fact that all the canaries can see each other can also be beneficial, especially in the breeding season. Canaries are gregarious avians and can often be induced to breed when they see others of their kind doing likewise. These metal units can be purchased in blocks, or you can purchase panels which can be clipped together to form any size of cage you wish.

The front of either type of cage will accommodate a metal

Canaries enjoy the company of their own kind. However, pet canaries should be kept in single cages because two males will fight during breeding season, and a male will not sing as much if housed with a female.

finch cage front. The bars on these are narrower than on those used for budgerigars, and the door slides up and down rather than opening downward. They contain two or three holes which are head holes so the birds can feed from externally mounted feeder pots. These are not essential as you can as easily use internal feeders, or automatic dispensers that clip to the outside and release seed into a tray inside the cage. If you make your own cages, it is wise to check on the cage front sizes prior to constructing a cage.

The base of the cage should contain a sliding tray that can be removed for cleaning. This can be covered with paper, sawdust, wood shavings, or any other absorbent material. Sawdust is rather messy and can irritate a bird's eyes, stick to the food, cause bronchial problems and tends to clog in corners when it is damp. Wood shavings are better, but still messy. Brown paper is this author's choice as it presents no problems, and is easy to remove.

The cages can be painted with either a gloss or an emulsion. Be sure the paint is lead free. Normally, exteriors are painted black with the interior in white, or an attractive pastel shade. However, you could use a light color for the exterior as well and make the birdroom more cheerful.

Plastic cages are becoming more popular because they can easily be mass produced and are readily cleaned. Plastic is often used more so for pet cages than for breeder units (these usually being made of metal).

Apart from the cages used in the birdroom you will of course need special cages if you plan to exhibit your canary. You will also need one or more small cages that you can use for transporting your birds. Most breeders will use the Gloster canary or Zebra finch type exhibition cage as a

A clear plastic bath may be attached to the door of your canary's cage. Baths may even be attached to a breeding cage because breeding birds must bathe often to keep their eggs at the proper humidity level.

transport unit, but any cage that has a carrying hole or handle will suffice.

FURNISHINGS & ACCESSORIES

The furnishings and accessories for the birdroom and cages range from perches to electrical fittings. The most useful fitting in the birdroom is some form of lighting. The favored choice being natural daylight fluorescent lamps. A wide range of coatings for fluorescent lights exist, so it will pay to discuss these with your local pet shop dealer. As mentioned, those emitting near to natural light are the best. Bear in mind that the coatings of these lamps wear off slowly, so that even though they may still be working, it is worthwhile to replace them about once a year.

You can have dimmer devices attached to fluorescent lights which are certainly worthwhile. You can also purchase light sensors that will switch the lights on whenever it gets too dark in the day (when it is very overcast), and at dusk. If you decide not to install these, do install a night light of low wattage in the birdroom. This removes the risk of night fright and saves the birds from panicking when you leave the birdroom and suddenly switch off the lights. Night fright is any sudden noise or any sudden noise or light that startles the birds and causes them to dash about in the dark, and maybe hurt themselves.

Canaries are hardy birds that are well able to cope with temperate climates. However, in the very cold periods they do appreciate some background heat—and you certainly will as well when attending to chores on those freezing winter evenings. There are thermostatically controlled furnaces specially designed for birdrooms. Some models even have built-in cooling fans for the summer as well. However, any form of controlled

heating will be fine, as long as it does not

All canaries enjoy a bath. An enclosed bath will help to keep the cage relatively dry. An open bath may also be used. Your local pet shop carries an assortment of baths, inquire which would be best suited for the type of cage you have.

release fumes or represent a fire risk. If you live in a very warm and humid climate, some form of air conditioning will be a good investment, but do not go overboard with this. As with heating, you only want to keep the birdroom comfortable—not like a hothouse or a refrigerator, which we humans are apt to do in our homes! Rapid fluctuation in temperature represents the quickest way of inducing chills in any bird species.

An ionizer is another very useful appliance in a birdroom. The models range from small ones that plug into a lamp holder, to those which plug into power sockets.

They release millions of negative ions which cling to particles of dust and bacteria and make them heavier, such that they fall to the floor. They are thus easily removed during daily cleaning. They also neutralize odors. The operational costs of these are negligible even though they must be left on twenty-four hours a day.

Hot and cold running water is another valuable asset that makes daily chores much easier to cope with. Provide yourself with good working surfaces, cupboards, and quality seed storage bins fitted with lids. The polythene trash bins sold in large stores are fine for seed storage, but obtain the high quality ones which are made of better materials or the less costly ones made of recycled plastics. If your birdroom is maintained at a sensible temperature, the risk of the bins "sweating" and damaging the seeds will be non-existent.

Cages are normally supplied complete with perches, but even so you should keep your own stock of these. The perches can be round, oval or square. Their diameter can range from $\frac{1}{4}$ -$\frac{1}{2}$ in. (62-1.25cm.), with $\frac{3}{8}$ in. (.95cm.) being a typical size. The advantage of having various thicknesses is to ensure that the birds are provided with plenty of exercise for their feet.

You could feature one of each size in the cages, or you could shave a thick perch so that its diameter is variable, and the birds can choose the part they find comfortable. You could also use natural branches from apple or similar trees. Plastic perches are also now available.

If your finances allow, you are advised to install an alarm system. This is becoming more and more a standard fitting in many birdrooms that contain a valuable collection of birds. Even remote TV cameras are not unknown as breeders try to protect their stock of birds, which may have taken many years of hard work to produce. Just how much enjoyment you obtain from your canaries will, to quite a large extent, depend on how well your birdroom is organized. In order to devote the maximum time to the birds, you need a clean, roomy place where everything is neatly stored, and where it is a pleasure to work.

AVIARIES

Without a doubt the best way to view and enjoy any captive bird is in a well designed aviary. Most breeders have their aviaries or flights attached to the birdroom. The birds gain entry to the birdroom via small pop holes and enter a variably sized internal flight. You could also have one large display flight built onto your birdroom, or a number of smaller ones, which would be the more common practice for breeders. The size of the flights is determined by the space and the amount of cash you can afford to put into the project. The potential design and furnishings of a flight are unlimited.

Here we will briefly consider a few basic recommendations.

Site: If you have a choice, the best site for an aviary flight is a protected location that gives the birds the benefit of the early morning sunshine.

Floor: Although earth is a natural surface, it holds numerous drawbacks. The

Outdoor aviaries can add beauty to your yard. It is always wise to inform your neighbors of plans to erect such a structure to avoid any hard feelings.

An indoor aviary or flight will allow you to house a number of birds in one space. Birds that live in a flight remain in good condition because they receive a great deal of exercise.

continual fecal droppings of both the canaries and wild birds will quickly saturate the earth making it a potential health hazard. It is thus difficult to keep clean. It may not drain well, so after a heavy rain you may find it a very messy place to work in if this need arises.

A better surface would be gravel, which can at least be hosed and raked over. Better still are slabs or concrete. These can easily be hosed down and you can build them at a slight slope so that rain is carried away from the birdroom. They also make it difficult for rodents and other creatures to burrow into the flight. A concrete floor also provides an excellent base onto which you can erect the aviary structure, or build a small wall to take this.

The Flight Frame: The most practical way to erect a flight is to assemble it in panels over which weld wire is stapled. The suggested minimum thickness of the wooden timber frame is 2x1 in. (5x2.5 cm.). The frame should be well protected with preservatives before the weld wire is attached to it. By assembling panels, it is much easier to make extensions later on (or repairs should these be required). If you have many birds of prey, snakes, or mammals in your area, it is wise to

Branches from natural trees and live plants can be incorporated into your flight or aviary. Birds enjoy pecking over these.

build a double roof to the aviary. This prevents these predators from getting a hold of the birds. A 6 in. (15 cm.) space between the two roofs should suffice. From an esthetic viewpoint you will find that it is best to make the minimum height of the flight at least 6.5 ft. (1.98 m.).

The weld wire should be of 19 gauge (thickness), and have a hole size of ½ x ½ in. (1.25 x 1.25 cm.). Although a hole size of 1x1 in. (2.5 x 2.5 cm.) is less costly, it is not as good for preventing the entry of small mice and snakes. You can purchase weld wire that is coated with epoxy resin in black,

white, or green. This is very attractive but much more expensive.

If you include a door in the aviary to your garden, it is best to protect this with a safety porch as discussed for the birdroom. You may also find it useful to feature a number of removable corrugated or flat Plexiglas panels on the flight. One on the roof near the birdroom will provide a covered area that the birds can sit under on rainy days; it will also provide welcome shade on hot days. Panels can also be used to protect any exposed sides of the flight during inclement weather.

The pop hole

entrance to the birdroom should have a landing platform just below it, as well as a slide or drop door so that the birds can be retained in the flight or the birdroom as needed. It is easy to contrive a means of being able to open and close this door from outside of the aviary—which will be found very convenient at times.

The flight furnishings should include perches placed to allow the canaries the maximum possible flying space. A shallow bathing dish will also be appreciated in the warm weather, both for the birds to bathe in and to drink from. Shrubs can be planted in tubs, and a box of grass or soil will be well used by the birds for pecking over.

PERMISSIONS

Once you have designed your birdroom and aviary it would be advisable to check if you will need any local planning permissions to erect the structure. If any brick or concrete is to be used in its construction, this may be regarded as a permanent building, in which case it may affect the assessed value of your home. Local authorities may have regulations regarding any services you supply to the building. These may have to be inspected to ensure they meet all safety regulations. It would also be advisable to

The shape of an aviary can be any that you desire; a rectangular shape is most often used because it gives the birds the maximum of flying space.

mention your plans to your neighbors if the birdroom will be in close proximity to their yard or garden. It is unlikely they would object to a canary collection, but it does save any bad feelings or objections after the building has been erected.

Red-factor canary. Today, canaries are available in a much wider variety of colors and postures than most people believe. When purchasing any pet, health is the most important factor of any decision.

Stock Selection

If you are not only to be only a first time canary owner, but also a first time bird owner, there are a number of considerations that you must make before purchasing stock. These are as follows:

1. What sort of canary

Be sure you have had a good selection of birds before you make your choice. There are numerous varieties of canaries to choose from at your local pet shop.

do you want?

2. Why do you want a canary—for example is it to be a pet, an aviary bird, a potential exhibition bird, or part of the foundation stock for breeding?

3. How can you tell if it is healthy?

4. Where is the best place to obtain the sort of stock you want?

5. Are age and sex important to your choice?

6. Is there a best time of the year to purchase a canary?

The answers to these questions should give you plenty to think about before any purchases are made.

Gold agate opal canary. If you are looking for breeding stock, try to inquire about the bird's genetic background so that the desired offspring can result.

CHOOSING THE CANARY VARIETY

There are probably many more canary varieties than you thought there were, so you should first try to see as many of these as possible. This applies even if you are only

Dilute green frosted canary. The best way to see the most varieties in a single day is to visit a caged bird show.

wanting a single pet bird. Many of the varieties are illustrated in this book, but nothing really compares with seeing the living bird. Some can be seen in pet shops, and the rarer breeds can be obtained for you by the pet shop dealer. The best way to see most varieties in a single day is to visit a caged bird show, preferably one that is devoted to canaries. Such shows are advertised in the bird magazines of your country. Pet shops might also be able to advise you of forthcoming shows in your area.

You will find that there is great variation,

Lizard canary. Some of the rarer breeds are not as commonly found in pet shops. However, your dealer probably would be able to stock them for you upon request.

both in size and shape, of the differing varieties. There is also a wide selection of colors to choose from, especially in the new colored varieties (birds bred specifically for their color). The singing ability of canaries also differs from one variety to another, with certain breeds excelling in their song.

PET, AVIARY, EXHIBITION OR BREEDING BIRDS

There are four

categories of birds, and each differs in their requirements, from your standpoint. The pet or aviary bird does not need to be of any particular quality, assuming it is a nice typical example of its variety. Indeed, it may even be a crossbreed.

The pet bird should ideally be young, a requirement that is not as important in an aviary bird that is to be part of a mixed finch collection. The exhibition bird will fall into one of two types. That which is young and showing potential,

Border and Lizard canary. During the breeding season, birds will often begin to peck at other birds to collect feathers for their nest. It is often best to separate such birds.

and that which has already been exhibited with varying degrees of success. The proven winner will obviously be more costly than one which has been shown, but has not displayed

great success. The show bird obviously must be of good quality—which does not necessarily mean it will be a good breeding bird. The potential or actual breeding bird will be one which may not display all of the qualities needed for it to be a show stopper, yet will have obvious merit. It will not have bad faults, and its ancestry will be such as to suggest it should produce some stock that will be at least as good as itself,

Left: The crested canary appeals to many simply because it looks different than the common canary. **Opposite:** Developed in Italy, the Fidrino is one of the better known crested frilled canary varieties.

All of the different color varieties we know today have resulted from mutations of the wild canary and through crossbreedings

are a long way past their prime.

SELECTING HEALTHY STOCK

To a large extent you can determine the health of the stock you purchase by studying the person selling it and the conditions under which the stock is kept. If a person maintains the stock under hygienic conditions, and has an established record with canaries, it is most unlikely that anything other than a fit bird would be sold. When purchasing, your initial attention should therefore be directed at the general conditions you see before you.

The birdroom or store should be neat and tidy, with no smells or signs

hopefully better. Proven producers of quality chicks will clearly be more costly than young hopefuls. However, you do not want adults which that cleaning is not a high priority. The cages should be very clean, with no hardened fecal matter evident on the perches, or on the floor. The feeder dishes should be spotless, and with adequate seed and water in them. The birds should not be overcrowded in cages.

If you are not confident in the seller, then walk away. Even though you are satisfied that the seller will not try to sell you an unfit bird, you must still know how to judge if a bird is unhealthy. Any bird which has a problem will display some of the following external signs:

1. An ill bird will sit on its perch with its feathers all fluffed out.

Both of its feet will be grasping the perch, and its head will be tucked into its neck or be drooping forward. A healthy bird sleeps with its head tucked into its

Color is not always of the same intensity, thus many variations exist.

Color and type of a pet canary are two factors that are a matter of preference when choosing a bird. Very often those birds that are different than the average appeal most to the public.

neck and feathers fluffed, but will perch on one leg. It is usually other signs that, together with the bird's stance, indicate a problem. If a bird is huddled in the corner of a cage, it may be ill or it may simply be frightened.

2. Weeping eyes and a liquid discharge from the nostrils are clear signs of ill health.

3. A beak which is either cracked, or damaged could cause problems. Both mandibles should be neatly aligned.

4. There should be no clogged fecal matter around the vent of the bird, nor staining, which would suggest a present or recent problem.

5. The feathers of a fit bird will be tight to its body and display a good sheen. They should not

be coarse.

6. Bald areas indicate a problem, though missing feathers on the head of a young chick indicate its parents probably plucked these while it was still in the nest. This author would still pass over such a bird as there is no shortage of good youngsters from which you can select.

7. The flesh on either side of the breastbone should not appear hollowed. This condition is called "going light" and indicates a nutritional deficiency that is not easily rectified.

8. There should be four toes on each foot. Three facing forward and one backward. A missing or deformed toe may not bother a pet or aviary bird, but is totally undesirable in a show or breeding bird.

9. An ailing bird will

The rounded breast on these Border canaries shows good breeding potential of the variety.

Frosting results from the lack of color at the tips of the feathers; this is also referred to as non-intensive.

look listless and show no interest in food.

Finally, it can be mentioned that one or two broken or missing feathers should not put you off an otherwise lively and healthy looking canary. These will be replaced at the next molt, which happens each year in the late summer. The first molt takes place after youngsters are weaned, when they replace all the body feathers, but not the primary wing and tail feathers. Such birds are called unflighted. A year later they will shed and replace all of the feathers, after which they are termed flighted.

WHERE TO PURCHASE FROM

Your choice of where to obtain your initial canaries will be influenced by the reason you want them. A nice pet or aviary bird can be obtained from your local pet or bird shop. These birds usually will not have been bred to be prize winners at a canary exhibition, but they are perfectly suitable as pets. In some regards—

Silver agate opal canary. The agate color variety is caused by the so called paling factor, which lightens pigment.

cost of stock, for example— they will be superior.

For exhibition or breeding stock you will need to contact a breeder of repute or inquire from your pet dealer if such stock can be purchased. Top knot stock will obviously be more expensive. You should always be honest with the seller and tell him or

The angular and high shoulders of this Belgian canary may appear abnormal to someone who is not familiar with the breed.

her exactly what you are looking for, and about how much you can afford to pay. Generally, you will get what you pay for because bargains in any cage birds of quality are few and far between.

When visiting exhibitions you can make numerous contacts for purchasing stock, and often you may find that some of the birds on display are for sale.

AGE & SEX

If you are purchasing a bird as a pet, you should obtain a youngster. Not only will it have all of its life ahead of it, but it will more readily adjust to your home environment. A good age will be anywhere from about 6 - 9 months. For an aviary resident, age is not so important, though obviously you do not want a bird that is very old. Once a bird has its adult plumage you cannot really tell how old it is unless it carries a closed and dated metal leg band. Generally, if the scales on its legs are very hard and a little flaky, this would suggest it is no youngster.

As far as the exhibition or breeding bird goes, it really is a case of exactly what you want and how much you are prepared to pay to get it. Young, proven stock of high quality can command a very high price. It may often be over priced for no other reason than the breeder does not really want to sell it, so he or she asks a price that would put most people off. High quality stock that is maybe three or more years of age may be available at a very fair price. Such birds are perhaps surplus to the breeder's needs, as he or she has younger stock to breed from. Once a bird passes five years of age it is regarded as being past its prime—but may still produce quality youngsters. Do not dismiss such birds; they could represent excellent value for money. Use them as partners to younger stock.

Regarding the bird's sex, the pet owner will want a male because of its singing ability. This may apply to the aviary owner as well. As far as exhibitors and breeders are concerned, the sex is not important. Although you may hear that birds of a certain sex have greater capacity to pass on their virtues, you can generally forget such claims. It is true that a bird of either sex can be prepotent, but genes are passed equally from each sex at fertilization, and prepotent stock is rare. It is thus more a case of whether the birds you need have the features required. If they have, their sex, per se, does not matter.

Obviously you will need birds of both sexes for establishing your initial breeding stock. It does not matter which sex provides this or that virtue, as long as the virtues are there to be perpetuated.

WHEN TO PURCHASE

If you have good accommodation awaiting your initial stock, it does not really matter what season of the year it is when you purchase it. The more important factor is obtaining the right stock when the opportunity presents itself. You will find that pet shops have stock year 'round, as do breeders. However, if you plan to place the birds in an aviary, the spring is a good time to do this. This gives the birds longer and warmer days. If you wish to breed in your first year of keeping canaries, you will need stock in the very early spring in order to have time to condition them.

Very often, the single bird owner enjoys the hobby so much that a second and even a third bird is purchased.

This still gives you little time to really prepare the birds. It is important to remember to never rush into breeding until you have gained practical experience in keeping canaries in a fit, healthy state.

A good, balanced, and varied diet will result in fit and healthy stock.

Nutrition

Canaries are seed-eating birds. Most people know this, but far fewer people appreciate just how important other foods are to these birds. Breeding birds need a very wide ranging diet to produce chicks as well as to rear healthy youngsters. We can therefore look at nutrition in two parts: the seed diet and the non-seed part of the diet. First, we will look at nutrition with respect to feeder dishes and general husbandry terms.

FEEDING UTENSILS

A wide variety of feeding utensils exists from which you can

Canaries enjoy eating all types of greens. Too much will result in loose droppings; these should be rationed.

choose. Automatic dispensers are available in various sizes and models. Such dispensers are advantageous because much time is saved which would otherwise be devoted to checking and filling open dishes. These also keep the seed free of dust and spilled water. On the negative side, the very fact that you do not spend time watching the birds feeding may mean you do not notice the first signs of ill health, one of which is when a bird looses interest in its food.

For breeders, automatic dispensers are now the most popular means of containing seeds. Choose one with a good sized opening to the tray as this greatly reduces the risk of the seeds clogging the outlet hole. As a further precaution you should tap the dispensers several times each day to be sure the seed is falling into the tray. Water can be supplied via such dispensers as well. Be sure to clean these thoroughly on a regular basis. Water should be replaced daily.

Open feeder pots are still preferred by some breeders. These can either be of the type which hook onto the cage bars, or crock (earthenware) dishes placed on the cage floor. They must be blown over daily in order to remove the husks

Natural branches from fruit trees (except cherry) can be featured in your bird's cage or aviary. The leaves should be included so that these can be pecked over.

which can make it appear as though there are plenty of seeds when there are actually only empty shells.

All birds tend to be wasteful feeders, throwing out seeds not wanted initially in order to get to their favorites.

In addition to a varied seed diet, canaries appreciate an assortment of fruits and vegetables.

Such waste will not really be too costly for the pet bird owner, but can add up to quite an item for the breeder. With this in mind it is often best for the breeders to supply differing seeds in separate containers. You do not have to apply this to every seed type, but feed the main seed, canary, in its own dispenser, and maybe use one, at most, two, open pots in which to supply the seeds fed in much smaller quantities.

Small finger or egg drawers can be purchased in which to supply softfoods. These are fitted to the cage bars, or you could use small pots as used for seed. Wild plant or nesting material holders, which look like miniature horse hay racks, could be used for leafy plants and vegetables. They too are clipped onto the cage bars.

If you plan to keep a number of canaries in a colony system, or as part of a mixed bird collection in an aviary, you can purchase inverted jar seed feeders, or the chicken type seed hoppers. These allow a lot more seed to be contained within them.

FEEDING HUSBANDRY

The first thing that should be said about feeding your canaries is that seed must be available to them at all times—as must water and grit. They cannot store quantities of food in their digestive system as we can, so are continually feeding during the daylight hours. If you have only a few canaries, your pet shop can supply packaged, mixed canary seed, or sell you mixed seed by weight. If you have a collection of canaries, you will find it more economic to purchase your seed from the pet shop. The seed should be dry and free of dust, and have no musty smell to it.

Like any other food, seed is perishable and will quickly loose its value unless stored correctly. A dry container should be used. Do not be tempted to purchase too much seed at a time, it is better that you have a steady supply of fresh seed than that which has been in your birdroom for months. Seed, even of the same variety, varies considerably in its quality depending on many factors. These include its country of origin, the soil it was grown in, when it was harvested, and how long it has been stored. These factors will be reflected in its price, so always choose the best quality (which will prove the most economic in the long run). Your birds will gain more nutritional benefit from this.

Softfood and plant matter has a very short life. As a general guide,

Fruits, vegetables, and berries may be chopped up into small pieces to make it easier for your birds to eat, or they may be left in their natural form.

feed only what the birds will consume in about two hours. Wash all plant matter before feeding in order to remove any residual pesticides or other potential toxins that may be coating the plants. For aviary birds, softfood and plants are best supplied in the

One of the main constituents of a canary's seed diet is that of the bird's name, canary seed. This is how it naturally grows in the wild.

the vitamin content. Place the food in the protected part of the aviary so that it is shaded from the sun and not likely to get wet if it rains. The seed part of the diet would normally be supplied in the indoor shelter of the birdroom, but some breeders might supply this in a covered part of the outdoor flight.

If bunches of wild plants are to be placed in the aviary, they should be clipped to the weld wire and not suspended from the roof. Some finch species are able to cling to hanging plants with no problem, but canaries are not among these. Plants must be on a surface the birds can alight on without

early morning or late afternoon. Thus, they are not subjected to the heat and rays of the midday sun, which quickly reduces their value, especially that of having to perform acrobatics; this is the aviary mesh or the floor.

Remember that cracked feeder dishes are a potential health hazard, so always replace these as soon as damage is noted. It is wise to number the food

Hemp seed is favored by canaries. They should not, however, be permitted to gorge themselves on this.

and water containers such that the same pots are always placed back into the same cage after cleaning and filling. Where hygiene is concerned, you can never really be too diligent.

THE SEED PART OF THE DIET

The basic seed in the canary diet is that of the bird's name, canary seed. This elliptical shaped seed will provide anything from 50-80% of the seed ration, depending on the views of the breeder (and the likes of the bird). The other seeds which are popular with canary breeders are black rape, white and yellow millet, panicum millet in the form of sprays (millet on the ear), hemp, niger, and pin-head oatmeal. The potential range of seeds is unlimited when you take into consideration not only cultivated

Automatic feeders of this type are typical for canaries. Be sure the opening to the tray is large enough so that the seeds cannot become jammed.

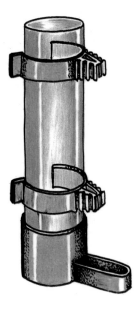

seeds, but also those of wild plants.

While canary and millet seeds will be readily accepted, birds differ considerably where other seeds are concerned. Much will depend on what the birds were accustomed to before you acquired them. During the breeding season a bird will prove more willing to accept foods that might ordinarily be passed over.

You will no doubt hear or read in the course of time that this or that seed is superior to others, or is of no value, or is disliked by canaries. These are the honest opinions of experienced breeders, but always remember that canaries are individuals, and that all edible seeds contain constituents of value to your birds. It is the ratio of one constituent to the other that changes both its taste and its value.

The value of a seed differs depending on what it is expected to achieve. If you want good growth in a youngster, it will need good protein seeds. During the cold weather a bird needs insulation in its skin, which can be provided by the fat rich seeds. Non-breeding birds in good health need only minimal protein and fat seeds, their metabolic needs being mainly that the food provides energy, which is derived from carbohydrate rich seeds. To this, foods that will provide the proteins and fats that are conducive to replacing tissue worn away by muscular activity are needed, as well as other vital ingredients that will maintain good health.

The dietary needs of an active aviary bird will clearly be different than those of a pet which is confined for long periods in a cage that is invariably too small for it to exercise in. Given these various facts you will appreciate that it is not possible to categorically state a canary needs this or that ratio of one seed to another. As a basic guide, I would supply a seed mix based on 65% canary seed, 20% rape, and 15% covering a mixture of other seeds which are rich in protein. This can then be adjusted up or down based on how the canaries look, and on which of the other seeds supplied the canary obviously enjoys. The wider the range of seeds that your birds will accept, the lower the risk that any one ingredient is missing.

Plantings can be supplied in foil trays and placed on the floor of your flight or aviary.

In reality, any quoted seed ratios have only limited value. This is because if seed is always available to your birds, as it should be, the fact that you supply, 50, 60 or 70% of canary seed is of no particular importance. If the bird consumes only the canary seed, which is replaced, it is thus eating 100% canary. In other words, the bird decides what percentage of one seed to another it will eat, not you. It is only by withholding, or adding, differing seed types that the canary does or does not

eat, that you can influence the actual consumed ratios.

You should be aware that birds, like people, do not always eat only that which is good for them. For example, if a bird gets "hooked" on millet sprays, it will gorge itself on these to the absence of other needed seeds. With this in mind you should limit any seeds, other than canary, which your birds seem to be unduly taking in preference to others.

SOAKED SEED

If you place a quantity of seed in a shallow dish of tepid water and keep this in a darkened cupboard for 24 hours the germination process will begin. This changes the constituent value of the seeds, and they also become much softer. Before feeding the soaked seeds to the birds, be sure to rinse them. Your birds will relish the seeds in this form and such seeds are very useful foods for young birds, unwell birds, and those which are recovering from an illness. However, do not overfeed soaked seed, and bear in mind that any not eaten after a couple of hours must be discarded, you cannot save them for another day.

If the seeds are soaked for an additional 24-48 hours, rinsed and placed in fresh water at the half way point, they should start

Your local pet store carries many types and package sizes of canary seed from which you can choose. Photo courtesy of Rolf C. Hagen Corp.

to send out small shoots. Again, these are especially enjoyed by birds. Apply caution in the feeding of germinated seeds because there is the possibility they may contain toxins at this point, depending on the plant species. A small quantity should not cause any problems.

NON-SEED FOODS

In the wild, canaries eat various foods as they come into season. These include fruits, some vegetable matter, and any insects and their larvae which are available to them. We cannot duplicate the actual items, but we can supply foods that contain much the same constituents. Indeed, commercial canary softfoods save us the time and bother of having to gather, cultivate, or prepare high protein foods, such as insects and mashes, which birdkeepers of not so many years ago had to do. Some breeders still prefer to make up their own softfoods using recipes handed down, or thought up by the individual. By so doing, they hope to keep feeding costs down, but whether this is achieved is very debatable if time

Spray Millet is very much enjoyed by all birds. Pet shops carry a large variety of this as well as other treats that will be appreciated by your bird. Photo courtesy of Hagen Products.

and the actual food value is taken into consideration.

You can purchase protein foods which may be given straight from the packet or after dampening with water. They come under various names, such as canary rearing food, softbill food, insectivorous food, egg biscuit meal, and so on. Check that the life of the vitamin part of the softfood has not expired—it will normally be printed on the packaging. Be sure to store the food as recommended by the manufacturer, otherwise its life will be greatly reduced.

Greenfoods, in the form of fruits and vegetables, can be supplied either as a mixed salad or as individual foods on differing days. Either way, chop them up into small pieces that a canary can cope with and place them in a small pot or a shallow container. The range is enormous and includes peas, lettuce, broccoli, brussels sprouts, spinach, potatoes, celery, oranges, and apples, as well as wild plants such as dandelion, chickweed, shepherd's-purse, plantains and their like. Wild plants can be given complete with their roots, the birds enjoy pecking over such plants.

Grain by-products, such as cereal flakes, together with dairy products, such as milk,

All greens and wild plants are relished by canaries and will be eaten in earnest until no more exist in the cage.

cheese, butter, and yogurt, are other items that can form part of a feeding regimen. Wholemeal bread soaked with milk is enjoyed by many breeding canaries and will help provide some of the essential calcium.

A number of specialized canary conditioning foods and tonics can be mixed with the regular diet or offered separately as treats. Photo courtesy of Living World.

Calcium can also be provided via powder sprinkled on seed or other food items, or via oyster–or eggshell duly crushed into small pieces. Cuttlefish bone is favored by many hobbyists as a source of calcium. Breeding birds need plenty of this, but you should not go overboard because too much can be as harmful as not enough. This fact applies to all minerals as well as to vitamins.

When you are preparing birds for the breeding period the protein part of the diet should be steadily increased commencing a couple of months before. It is no use to suddenly give the birds a pile of high protein foods two weeks before you expect them to go to nest. This will not achieve the desired results. It takes months for foods to be converted into the correct amount of muscle needed by breeding birds. High protein foods should be fed throughout the rearing period and then steadily reduced as the season draws to a close. All foods, other than basic seeds, should be supplied on a build up and slow down basis, never suddenly in a glut as this can cause problems.

FOOD SUPPLEMENTS

As a rule of thumb, if your birds look and move like healthy birds should, they will not require any food supplements. The exceptions are those varieties, such as the Norwich or colored canaries, that are traditionally color fed in order to enhance the color of the feathers. In such instances, you can purchase various color food supplements that are fed during the molting period, either mixed in with rearing foods, or by adding a liquid to the drinking water. Although, in theory, color feeding has no benefit once the molt is complete, the reality may be somewhat different. The color supposedly can only enter the feather shaft while it is receiving a blood supply,

Bright eyes and good feathering are indications that your bird is receiving a well balanced and nutritious diet.

Not all birds go through a complete molt at one period. This means that some feathers may be shed after the main molt is complete. Likewise, any feathers lost after a molt may be replaced. If color feeding is stopped completely, it is probable that the newer feathers will be a differing color. It is therefore wise to continue color feeding on a dilute scale if you are an exhibitor. If you keep both color and non-color fed varieties, be sure to segregate these during the molting period so you can feed accordingly.

You must experiment with the amount of coloring agent supplied because an excess will spoil the colors and make them brassy or too reddish.

A final comment regarding color feeding is that you should not assume this is the last word on the color of your birds. Color is the end result of a complex chain of reactions that combine chemical, genetic, and environmental factors. Light and temperature both affect color, as does the bird's genetic background. You must consider all of these factors in order to obtain maximum color, rather than rely on coloring agents.

Grit is not a supplement in the general sense of the term, but an essential additive. Having no teeth, birds crush seed with their beaks or swallow it whole. Grit is needed to mix with the seed and helps to grind it to a pasty pulp that is readily absorbed into the bloodstream for distribution to the body cells. Purchase a small grit suited to canaries and ensure it is always available to them. Rock salt is another mineral that you may find of benefit to your birds.

Water

Water is essential to maintain good health in any animal species. Its quality is very variable, a fact that few breeders really appreciate.

Faucet (tap) water may well be suitable for us to drink, but it may be mildly toxic to such small creatures as birds. It may not kill them, but it is most certainly able to affect their health and the color and quality of their feathers. Apart from the chlorine and chloromide content, it may contain high levels of calcium, plus trace amounts of copper and various salts. It may even contain green-blue algae; these are toxic to fish so it can be assumed will not be good for a canary.

Ideally, if you are able to pass the water through a good filter system built into your faucet, you might be surprised at the positive results this brings forth in your birds. Often, birds which have access to rainwater will prefer to drink and bathe in this than in that which you might supply— which suggests they know which is best for them, and why a filter is a worthwhile investment (for yourself as well). Should you wish to test your water for its pH value, I would suggest that you want a reading of neutral to slightly acidic for your birds, this being especially so of water used to spray their feathers with. You can purchase tablets that will remove the chlorine and other impurities from water. These can be obtained from your pet or aquatic stores.

Canaries enjoy bathing in cool water, early in the day. Bathing dishes can be purchased that sit on the floor, or one that attaches to the side of the cage may also be used.

Good nutritional husbandry is a case of blending a basic knowledge of the value of various foodstuffs with a goodly amount of common sense and a willingness to experiment now and then. It must be combined with all other areas of husbandry and if the result is a healthy looking bird that reproduces strong healthy chicks, then you are doing just fine.

Lizard canary feeding newly hatched chicks. This mother Lizard canary will be kept very busy over the next few weeks feeding her young.

Practical Breeding

If you are a first time birdkeeper, the first and best advice you can be given is to befriend an experienced breeder; preferably of canaries, but one specializing in finches will be almost as good. Such a person will be invaluable to you if you should experience problems—or even if you do not. It is one thing to read about breeding in a book, but the reality always brings forth little queries that may not be covered in a text.

Yorkshire canaries. Canaries tend to become aggressive during the breeding season. It is wise to keep the males in individual cages to avoid conflicts.

SELECTING BREEDING STOCK

Regardless of the quality of your initial stock, it must be very healthy. While it would be very nice if the newcomer could go out and purchase the very best birds, this would not only be very

Good breeding stock is essential to obtain vigorous offspring. Female canaries should be extremely fit before permitted to raise a clutch of young.

expensive, but not really the wisest path to take. You will obtain far greater satisfaction from upgrading your stock over the years, than from starting off with the best, which is the result of someone else's skills, and trying to maintain the quality. This does not mean you want to start with rubbish, because with this you would probably give up birdkeeping before you could upgrade it!

The happy medium is a small nucleus of well bred birds that may not be eye openers, but are very sound for most of their features. It is important that they come from a line of birds which have a proven record for both

Canaries do not have much of a mating ritual. The male will sing to the female, and when she crouches down in response, she is ready for him to mate her.

breeding to their type, and producing vigorous offspring.

The chosen supplier of your birds will ideally be someone within your locality, so that they can be the friend mentioned earlier. You will probably need more of their birds once you are underway. Good sound birds will not cost you a fortune, but neither will they be as inexpensive as pet birds. Be prepared to pay a fair price; after all, you will no doubt want the same consideration when you come to sell your stock. It costs as

It is better to have hens that are less than 3 years old as breeding stock. Males are best between 2 and 5 years of age.

much to feed mediocre canaries as it does good ones, so start with sound stock.

You may be offered birds that are a little older than the ideal, but such stock can be very useful. In particular, a quality male is the favored choice, not because he can transmit more of his qualities in a single mating, but because he can mate with a number of hens in a single season. He can thus perpetuate his quality more rapidly than can a hen. Further, it is better to have younger hens so that they have the vigor needed to produce strong chicks. The ideal is thus a few good males, which may be 2-5 years of age, plus a number of hens, preferably those which have already raised chicks so their parental ability is known, and the quality of their offspring likewise.

You want all of your stock from the same breeder, at least initially, because if you start mixing genes (blood lines), the quality

Young Gloster canaries. Raising canaries is a truly rewarding experience. After a year or two of breeding, you may want to experiment with some of the lesser seen varieties.

achieved by each of the breeders selling you stock may not be reproduced in the offspring of such unions. Once you have a year or two of experience, and have studied methods of breeding, you may then look to other breeders to provide stock that might be able to improve features that are lacking in your birds. However, before that stage is reached you should first explore the potential within the gene pool you commence with.

HOW MANY BIRDS?

It is all but impossible to advise you on how many birds to keep because it comes down to how much cash you

Border canary pair. The Border canary is a very prolific breeder. It is advised that this be the variety for those who are beginning the canary breeding hobby.

It is best to begin a breeding program with a small number of birds. As you gain experience, you can increase your stock.

have, and how much you are prepared to invest into your birdroom, cages, flights, equipment, and stock. Even if cash is not a major problem, it is best to start in a small way. For one thing, you may decide after a season that you prefer to keep cockatiels! You may find you do not have the enthusiasm you started with, or you may find that your initial stock was not as good as was hoped. All of these reasons suggest that the prudent course is a few birds. This will give you the flexibility to change without undue problems, or losing too much invested money. This

so, a small stock of two or three males and maybe six hens should give you plenty to work with, and more than enough problems to cope with without getting unduly overwhelmed. A smaller number than this is fine, especially if this means you can commence with better birds than if you try to stretch your cash into too many.

Apart from your initial stock, you will be wanting nesting pans, spare cages, more seed, and of course a lot of time— so bear these things in mind when you start so you do not find you have overstretched your resources.

BREEDING CONDITION

The importance of this state cannot be over emphasized. Do not expect to be able to purchase birds and have them breeding within a few weeks. Even if the supplier kept his or her stock in hard condition, the change of environment will take the birds some weeks to adjust. While it was stated earlier in the book that it is not so important when you purchase your initial stock, this is not quite true of potential breeding birds. These I would suggest a beginner purchases in the late summer or autumn. You then have the winter to gain practical management experience, and bring your stock into condition for breeding in the spring.

To do this, the birds should have as much time in an aviary, or at the very least in a good sized indoor flight, as possible. At this time they will be given a basic seed diet, but as the breeding season starts to approach, an increase in the protein element of the food should be given. The build-up of these foods can commence about 8 weeks before breeding is anticipated. At this same time the sexes can be separated—the cocks into individual cages, but the hens can be left together in a flight so they have the maximum time to exercise.

FINAL PREPARATIONS

About four weeks before breeding commences it is wise to treat all breeding stock for parasites, such as mites. Powders or aerosols can be used, with the treatment being repeated as directed on the packaging. All nest material should likewise be treated as this will greatly reduce the risk of an infestation when the birds have chicks. If mites are seen on chicks, they should be treated. Failure to do so can result in the hen abandoning them, or the chicks becoming greatly emaciated.

The nails of the birds should be checked at this time for their length. Any that are overgrown should be trimmed so the risk that they will accidentally scratch the eggs is reduced. The vent feathers of cocks can also be checked for excess length and trimmed if need be.

NESTING PANS, MATERIALS AND EGG DRAWERS

Canaries use an open nest pan which can be made of plastic, wicker, wire, or crock (earthenware). This is lined with a felt or foam pad. Each of these items can be purchased from your pet shop. The nest pan is usually located in the breeding cage, where it is securely screwed or hung onto a side or back wall. Alternatively, you can purchase nest pan holders which are hung onto a door of a double door cage. One of the doors is fastened in the open position and the nest pan is placed into the holder which, being external, allows the birds more room in their cage. This is beneficial because you are more easily able to inspect and attend to the chicks if this is needed.

The felt or foam can be secured onto the pan with glue, or can be secured with fine string or similar material which is threaded through the holes

"Dummy" eggs are used to ensure that a clutch of chicks all hatch within one or two days of each other.

usually found in commercial nest pans. The actual nesting material can be dried moss or grass, or any of the man-made materials sold for nesting by pet shops. This is placed into the cage and the canary will fashion the nest from this. It is worth pointing out that as canaries use an open nest you must be sure this is not subjected to direct sunlight— this is more likely with external pans than those inside the cage. During the breeding period you can arrange for suitable shade if you see direct sunlight could be a problem.

You will need an egg storage drawer on hand for when the eggs are laid. This is simply a shallow box with lined compartments large enough to take about 5-6 eggs. You do not have to remove the eggs from your canaries, but this is a standard practice that ensures the chicks all grow at the same rate. If allowed to incubate them naturally, the first chicks to hatch will receive more food and attention than the last ones, which might be neglected. The eggs can be marked with a felt tipped pen so you know which eggs are from which pair.

BREEDING REGISTER

You will need a breeding register which can be obtained from clubs, or you could devise your own. The object of this is to ensure you record all details from each pairing. Thus you will want to know which birds were paired, when, how many eggs were laid, when hatched, how many survived to independence, their colors, and any other notes on them. This history of your stock will be essential for your future planning, and will provide back reference in the event you wish to trace any information.

LIGHT AND HEAT

Birds can be induced to breed throughout the year if suitable light and heat is supplied. It is not recommended that beginners breed during the colder winter months. Even in the early spring it may be found that some extra light and heat is needed in certain temperate regions. The birdroom temperature should not be allowed to fall below 50° F (10°C)—but you also do not want it unduly hot, just comfortable. By the time the birds have paired, and are ready to rear the chicks, the lighting should be provided about 14-15 hours a day. This is spread between both natural daylight and artificial.

INTRODUCING THE PAIRS

About a week before planned matings, the

Breeding birds require extra protein during the breeding season. Darker greens and vegetables such as spinach and escarole, as well as some type of canary rearing food, should be supplied prior to the laying of the eggs.

the cock can commence feeding the hen. The wire slides are better because they allow maximum vision between the birds of a pair. This is important in bringing the birds into final condition. By keeping them separated, you are able to satisfy yourself that both birds are compatible and anxious to pair with each other.

Actually, not until the partition is separated will you be totally sure that the pair is compatible. If they squabble, you should separate them and try again each day for 2-3 days. If they still do not get along, you can assume one or the other just doesn't like your choice of partners

pair can be placed in a double breeding cage with the slide partition in place. If the slide is of wood or Plexiglas it should be drilled with holes of at least ½ in. (1.25 cm.), so the birds can see each other, and for them. This so, try other pairings and success will usually follow. You can of course pair a male with two or three hens. In this case keep the hens in separate cages and introduce the male to each in turn.

Courtship involves the female calling to the male and carrying bits of nesting material in her beak. The male will sing to his mate, who will sit on her perch inviting him to mate her. In order to mate the hen, a male must be able to gain a good grip on the perch, which is why it is important that he has all of his toes present. If his grip is lacking, he may appear to mate the hen, but fail to do so. It should be pointed out that just because you see birds mate, it does not mean it has been successful. Either of the pair may not be fertile, or the mating may not have taken if you know that both are proven birds. In such an instance the hen may well act as though all is well and she will proceed to lay eggs, but these will be "clear," meaning unfertilized.

EGG LAYING AND INCUBATION

The average size clutch laid by a canary is four, but this can range from one to six. As the eggs are laid (each day) they are normally removed and placed in an egg drawer. These should

A hen canary will sit diligently on her eggs. She may only come off of the nest to feed herself.

be kept where the temperature will not fluctuate much. As the eggs are taken they are replaced with artificial ones made of china or plastic. These can be purchased from pet stores, or those specializing in avicultural supplies. When the hen lays her fourth egg (or in theory should lay such an egg), you can replace the original eggs, and remove the dummies.

The hen will then sit on the eggs in earnest. The incubation period will be approximately 14 days. This can take one or even two days longer if the ambient temperature is on the low side, or it could be 13 days if it is somewhat warm. The male is usually

Each egg a hen canary lays becomes progressively darker. The last egg is almost entirely specked with brown.

removed from the breeding cage once a mating is thought to have taken place, so he can be mated to other hens. If there are no other hens to be mated most breeders will still remove the male, though this is not essential as most males make good parents. In the event that he has been removed and the hen seems reluctant to sit on the eggs, he should be reintroduced. This will usually overcome the hen's obvious concern over her missing mate.

FERTILITY AND EGG TRANSFER

After about a week from having placed the eggs back under the hen they can be checked for their fertility. This is done by very gently holding them up to a strong light source, such as a light bulb, or by using one of the pencil torches now available for this purpose. If the egg appears opaque, or is dark at one end only,

The average size of a canary clutch is four, but this can range anywhere from one to six.

this indicates it has not been fertilized (is clear), or was fertilized but the embryo has died. A fertile egg will appear dark throughout.

The dead in shell, or clear eggs, can be destroyed and the fertile eggs replaced to the nest.

If only one or two eggs are fertile, and you have other hens sitting on eggs, you have the option of fostering. It may happen that another hen has only one or two fertile eggs, in which case you can transfer the eggs of one to the other. The hen which thus has no eggs left will be wanting to go to nest about a week later, and can be mated again. In this way, you obtain the maximum number of eggs from your hens.

If no other hens are available, your option is to let the hen finish incubating the one or two eggs, or discard them in the hopes the second round of eggs will contain three or four fertile eggs, as can sometimes happen. If you do foster eggs to another hen it is better that such a hen be a different color. In this way you will know which are her chicks and which are the fostered ones. This assumes you are aware of the genotype of the two hens, and can be sure from theoretical expectations which colors can and cannot come from the hens.

HATCHING PROBLEMS

At the end of the incubation period the chicks will hatch by breaking through the shell using their "egg tooth". This is a special growth on the upper mandible of the beak which disappears once the chick is free of its shell. Sometimes, due to the shell being very thick, or the chick rather weak; it is unable to break the shell, or having broken a hole, it seems unable to make further progress. In either case the chick will die if it cannot break through after a reasonable lapse of time.

If the egg is "pipped", meaning a small hole is seen but no progress has been made over a few hours, you can very gently remove a piece of the shell around the hole and then leave matters for a while longer to see if this helps. If not, you can remove more of the shell. The chick may die, but you have at least given it a chance to survive. If an egg has gone two days past its due hatching date, you can also try to gently break the shell to see if this helps. It may be that the chick is already dead, but this is not always the case.

BANDING CHICKS

Once all of the chicks are free of their shells, the shells will either fall out of the nest, or be eaten by the hen. By this stage the hen should be receiving plenty of rearing food and a small amount of greenfood.

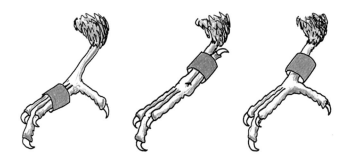

By the 5th to 7th day after hatching, the canary chicks can be banded with closed, coded, metal rings. This illustration demonstrates the proper way to band your birds.

The chicks grow rapidly and by the 5th-7th day they can be fitted with closed, coded, metal rings. These are obligatory if you wish to exhibit canaries in some countries, but not in others, including the UK. You should check this out with the local club of your country. The rings are sold by some pet shops, all clubs, or from the manufacturers who advertise in bird magazines. Be sure to obtain the correct ring size for your canary variety.

Many bird breeders do not fit closed rings because they feel they are a potential danger to the bird. There is truth in this fear, though it is not as bad as sometimes thought. The hen may

Border canary pair. Sometimes a male canary will not like the way a female has arranged the nest, and will pull out all of the material leaving the hen to rebuild.

eject the ring (thus the chick) from the nest because, to her, the ring is unwanted rubbish cluttering her tidy nest. A ring can become clogged with fecal matter and cut off the blood supply to the chick's toes, but this is only possible if the breeder neglects inspection and cleaning duties. Finally,

once a chick has fledged, the ring can get caught on a fine branch or protruding strands of mesh in the aviary. Such accidents are actually relatively rare, and often the breeder is able to free the bird before any serious damage is done.

The alternative to the closed ring is a split celluloid ring. This can be fitted to a bird of any age, though it cannot act as clear proof of a bird's age or ancestry as can the closed ring. Such rings are available in various single or double colors and make excellent temporary identification tags. Fitting a ring is done by gently pressing the chick's outer toe backwards so it is parallel with the leg, then gently sliding the ring over the other three toes until it clears the backward facing toe. If you are unsure about this, have a breeder show you. It is easy as long as you are careful. Split rings have a special tool to help open and fit the ring.

If the closed ring falls off the chick, try it again each day until it stays on. If you are too late in trying to fit a ring do not be tempted to force this on, just leave the chick without this type of ring.

CHICK REARING

By the time the chicks are about 13-16 days old, they will be well covered with feathers, and within 7-10 days of being weaned. Weaning is the process whereby the chicks stop being fed by their parents (or hen as the case may be) and are able to feed themselves. At about the end of their second week, the normal practice with many canary breeders is to place the chicks' nest pan into a corner of the cage and fit a new one in its original place. Fresh nesting material is

Canary chicks 1 and 2 days old. At this age chicks only beg for food and sleep.

supplied to the hen and she will begin building a new nest for her second round of chicks.

At this time the male can be reintroduced if he was removed previously (or another male can be used). The next clutch of eggs will be laid and the hen, if she is on her own, will not only incubate the second round, but will also continue to feed her first round chicks. If the male is retained with the hen, he will help feed the first round of youngsters, thus making life easier for the hen. The first round chicks can be separated from the hen when they are about three weeks old. It is wise to place them in a partitioned cage next to the hen so she can continue

Canary chick 7 days old. This canary chick has already been banded for identification.

feeding them through the wire bars of the partition. They can be given rearing softfood during this time, soaked and regular seed, as well as finely chopped fruits and greenfoods. They will of course need their own supply of water in a shallow dish as they tend to drink quite a lot. A flomatic water dispenser can be included so they get to know how these work. It is at this age that the feeding habits of the chicks are firmly embedded in them, which is why a varied diet is beneficial.

Neither the softfood nor the supplementary foods should be allowed to become soured; remove and replace that not eaten every few hours. Watch for the chicks that are eating well by themselves and

Canary chicks 6 and 7 days old. The first feathers are beginning to come out on these chicks.

these can be moved to a nursery cage. Do not remove chicks from the feeding care of their parents on set dates as some breeders may advocate, but base the time on when you know for sure the chicks are self sufficient.

At about six weeks of age the youngsters can be placed into a large indoor or aviary flight where they will begin their first molt. During this time, all the body feathers will be shed and replaced, but the primary wing and tail feathers will remain. These, as well as all other feathers, will be molted one year hence. Such first year birds are called unflighted, becoming flighted when the wing and tail feathers are shed and replaced.

It is during the molt that color feeding, if appropriate to the variety, is commenced. Molting is a very debilitating period for the chicks: so you should be especially watchful of them at this time. Make sure the molting youngsters have access to bathing facilities. The time it takes for the molt is very

At 12 and 13 days old the eyes of these chicks are now open.

variable as it is dependant on many factors, but it normally takes a number of weeks and can run into a few months. It is a gradual process in which the feathers of differing

Canary chicks 7 days old. A hen canary can feed a number of chicks. Sometimes, however, she may require assistance from the male.

areas of the body are lost, and replaced after which another area of feathers is molted, and so on until the process is completed.

BREEDING PROBLEMS

There are many things that can go wrong during the breeding period. Eggs may fail to hatch, and chicks may die in the shell or shortly after hatching. Hens may abandon the eggs, or they may eat them. The reasons for these happenings are numerous. They include nutritional deficiencies, hormonal imbalances, disturbances by the breeder, chilling, excessive heat, lack of humidity, hairline cracks in eggs, congenital hereditary conditions, and many other causes. These are beyond the scope of this text, so you are advised to discuss potential problems with breeders, as well as to seek out works devoted to avian disorders.

One condition, however, that should be mentioned here is that known as egg binding. This distressing and potentially fatal condition is seen in hens that are either not fully fit, or have suffered from a nutritional deficiency. It may also happen if the temperature is low, thus resulting in the hen's muscles being chilled and not able to contract and move an egg down the oviduct. The result is that the hen is unable lay the egg, which

becomes blocked in the oviduct. Unless it is removed, the hen may die from the exertion of trying to lay it.

The hen may be seen fluttering to the floor and be in obvious distress. The remedy is to immediately place her in a hospital cage and provide heat treatment. This usually enables her to release the egg as the heat relaxes her muscles. You may, before placing the hen in the hospital cage, gently smear olive oil on her vent region, which may also help. Be very careful when handling the hen as you do not want the egg to break within her. This may cause peritonitis, an infection of the reproductive tract.

If the egg is not

Weaned canary chicks can be kept together in a stock cage until their sex is known.

immediately if the egg fails to be released. The older canary is more likely to suffer from egg binding than is the young bird. Likewise, obese birds are prone to the condition because, like older birds, their muscle condition is not as it should be.

Once a bird has released the problem egg it may continue to lay other eggs. If no more are laid, it is best to place the hen into a flight cage and forget breeding her until the next season, when hopefully she will be in good, hard condition. Of course, if a hen has previously been egg bound and was regarded as being fit, it would be best not to use her for breeding as the

forthcoming within an hour or so, you could try to gently manipulate it from her, but this is a risky procedure. However, the alternative of doing nothing is also risky. Call your vet

Canary chicks grow at a very rapid rate. In another week these chicks will have most of their first feathers.

condition may, in that hen, have a genetic base.

Many of the problems encountered during the breeding season are attributable to the poor health of the adults, lack of adequate hygiene, and the failure of many novices to appreciate that even with domesticated birds like canaries, success is not guaranteed. You must take the business seriously and prepare very carefully for the breeding period.

Intensive red canary. The red coloration of a red-factor can be enhanced with special coloring agents that can be added to the bird's food.

Basic Genetics

The value of genetics, or the science of heredity, is significant to any canary breeder. By understanding the basic principles of the subject you will be more attuned to the importance of

Gloster canary whose crest radiates well. The crest should be circular and even in form. It should fall in a straight line from the bill to the back of the head with the eyes clearly visible.

selecting stock of known ancestry. You can then apply genetics to your breeding program, in relation to the color

The Border fancy canary is an elegant looking breed that does not have any of the characteristics of the posture type canaries that are so hard to breed for.

or appearance of your birds, or both. Such knowledge can save you many wasted matings based on pure chance. Genetics is actually based on the fact that you can calculate your chances of success in achieving many objectives, especially in relation to color.

Even if you had a scientific training on the subject, genetics in isolation of other factors has little value, which is why many canary breeders with no genetic knowledge are able to consistently produce top quality birds. The prerequisite of capitalizing on genetics is that you must first be able to recognize what is good and bad in your stock, and then be able to make sound selections from which to breed. You must also maintain breeding records, because no one's memory is that good that they can recall all the results of pairings made even over a relatively short period. Finally, a canary can only exhibit its genetic potential if it lives in an environment conducive to this—which means its accommodation, its feeding, and its general care are bringing out its best qualities.

As you will appreciate, genetics is an extremely complex subject if you care to delve thoroughly into it. Fortunately, understanding the basic principles is not so difficult, so the average birdkeeper is able to at least appreciate what happens when birds mate, and may even be able to apply the theory to a given objective. In this chapter we can only scratch the surface of the major principles, but hopefully enough that you can see the benefits of the subject.

GENES—THE VEHICLES OF INHERITANCE

Within the nucleus of all body cells are tiny structures known

as genes. These are arranged in a linear manner that may be likened unto a string of beads. The full "string" of genes is called a chromosome, and in all body (somatic) cells the chromosomes are found in pairs of equal length. In the sex cells one of a pair of chromosomes is shorter, and is termed the Y chromosome, the other being called the X. A cock canary has two X chromosomes, while a hen has one X and one Y (opposite of humans and all mammals).

Opposite: Red-factor canary. Frosting of a canary was once an undesired trait, Today, birds are bred especially for this type of feathering.

Genes act as units of coded information which tell the cells how to develop. There are many thousands of genes which collectively determine all features of the organism; the theory of genetics applying equally the same to all animals and plants. Some genes, termed major genes, are able to determine features in isolation of other genes, but most features are controlled by polygenes. This means they work on a collective basis, the more of a given gene an organism has, the more the feature will move either side of the average of the population. For example, let us imagine 20 gene pairs controlling body length. Some represent long length, others short length. If a bird had 10 pairs of each it would be the average size—but if it had more of one than the other this would be reflected in greater or lesser size.

It is not known how many pairs of genes control the many features that make up a bird, but the principles of genetics have long since been proved by experiments and the recording of millions of matings. It is a long and difficult process to apply genetics to bodily form, known as the phenotype, but color is more straight forward, so is invariably the feature used to explain the subject.

THE IMPORTANCE OF MUTATIONS

A mutation is a change in the way a gene expresses itself. It is the basis behind all varieties seen in both plants and animals. Mutations happen continuously in all animal species. Most are so minor that we never even notice them. Over thousands of years, however, they result in speciation—the formation of new species. The ones that interest us are those which are sudden and

A bird that is Dominant-white cannot be mated to another Dominant-white because this produces a lethal gene.

Gold agate opal canary. The opal mutation is the second canary variety with recessive inheritance — agate being the first.

these. We cannot create the mutation, because it is a random, natural happening whose cause is still not fully under-stood, but once it has appeared it can be retained and utilized.

very visible. Once a gene has mutated, it thereafter transmits its new expression in a predictable manner. By manipulating mutations we are able to create new varieties and new colors within

GENETIC LANGUAGE

In order to understand genetics you will have to become familiar with certain technical terms that form part of its language, just as you would if you were learning about car mechanics, computers, or any other subject. Let us look at the more commonly used terms.

Homozygous: This means two genes of a pair that impart the same instructions to the cells they are in. For example, if one is for brown coloration its opposite gene on the other chromosome will also be for brown.

Heterozygous: Here the two genes of a pair are for differing expressions. For example, one gene may be for a crest on the head, while the other may be for no crest. The two genes of a pair thus contain differing information that they will pass to the cells they are in. How this information is expressed is what genetics is about.

Allelomorph (Allele): This means the alternative expression of a gene. For example, crested is the allele of non-crested; it is the alternative gene to it at a given locus, in this instance the crest locus. A gene can have more than one allele, meaning it may have mutated more than once to create two or more alternative expressions to the original, or wild form of the gene. However, regardless of the number of alleles there are to a given gene the bird can only carry two genes for that feature at its locus.

Dominant: This means that the gene has the power to express itself when present in only single quantity. Crested is an example of this, as is dominant white. It is the power to express itself when present with any of its alleles.

Recessive: These genes need to be present in double dose before they are visually seen. If only one of a pair of genes is recessive you will not see its expression, but it will still be present in the bird.

The latter is said to be split for the recessive gene. When showing this in writing, the visual color is written first, and the recessive, or carried gene, is shown behind an oblique line. Thus a green bird split for brown would appear as green/brown. A bird can be split for a number of features at the same time, if they are carried at differing gene loci.

Locus (pl Loci): This is the particular position of a gene on its chromosome. There are many color loci, so there is one

Opposite: Whether Gloster fancy nestlings are coronas or consorts becomes apparent as they feather in.

for black, one for brown, one for dilution, one or two for white, and so on. Only by considering the expression of each gene at each locus can you determine what the colors of a given mating will result in. This is not quite as difficult as it may appear at first.

Genotype: The genetic make-up of a feature. For example, a green canary may be pure for green, or it may be carrying another color, which is not visible. Such birds have the same appearance (phenotype), but their breeding potential will be different as far as their color is concerned.

Normal: This is the wild type coloration or feature of a bird. For example, the wild type canary does not have a crest, so this is the normal bird as compared to the crested. If both birds of a pair of canaries were yellow, any calculations relating to normal would mean yellow. It is the color or feature that would be seen if the mutation that might affect it was not present.

ABBREVIATIONS (GENETIC SYMBOLS)

In order to make it easy to refer to a feature (i.e. color) when doing calculations of expectations, geneticists use abbreviations to represent the feature. These are as follows:

1. A capital letter is used to represent a dominant gene.

2. A lowercase letter is used to represent a recessive gene, or an unmutated (wild type) gene that is paired with a dominant mutation.

3. A dash is used to represent a gene of unknown status (i.e. whether it is a normal or mutated gene).

4. A small x is used to represent a mating or pairing.

5. A capital X is used to denote the X chromosome of the germ (reproductive) cells. A capital Y is used to represent the short female chromosome of the germ cells.

An explanation in the use of some of these terms will, hopefully, overcome problems often met by beginners to genetics. Let us use a self bird as an example (that is, a bird which exhibits melanin in all its feathers). Such a bird, which was homozygous for this color pattern, would have a WW genotype. A recessive white bird is one which carries no melanin, (i.e. it is a red eyed white (albino)). Such a bird would have a ww genotype, where w stands for the recessive mutation that causes pigment

Variegation results from the loss of melanin in some areas; this, in turn, is due to a mutation.

remember that W is the alternative gene to w—in a strict sense this means non-white, whatever that color may be. Once a mutation has been identified it can be given an abbreviation, in this case w for white. The normal gene to a mutation usually carries the same letter as the mutation. A bird with an opal feather pattern would be o, and the alternative normal to this would thus be O.

Now, it may happen that you have two self birds to breed from, but can you be sure they are homozygous,

not to form, i.e. white.

In this example you will note that the normal bird carries the same letter as the white mutant. This is in order that you that is WW? A bird that was Ww, thus carrying the recessive mutation for white, would look just the same as a purebreeding normal. In such a case your two selfs could both be WW, both be Ww, or one of each (i.e. a WW bird and a Ww). If you were asked what their genotype was you could not reply with certainty, so it would be written as W-, indicating the unknown gene. Only the results from their mating will establish what their genotype actually is.

BACK TO BASICS

With some terms and explanations now given we can return to the actual workings of genes. You will recall that genes are on chromosomes, and that the chromosomes are paired, each identical to the other, except in the sex cells. This so, a gene at a given locus on one chromosome has a partner on the other chromosome which is at the same locus. Both are for the same feature. A chick will inherit only one of the two genes from each parent, thus maintaining the paired situation. This, very much simplified, is because in the formation of sex cells the paired chromosomes divide. Now, if all of the genes on both sets of chromosomes of both parents were the same, it follows that the chicks will look just like their parents, other than for minor variations which are natural within the genes. This is in fact what happens.

However, if one of the parents carries a mutated gene, the mutated feature may eventually show up in future generations. Let us use the normal (self) bird and a mutant carrier of recessive white to see how things develop.

AUTOSOMAL RECESSIVE MUTATIONS

In this instance it does not matter which bird (i.e. cock or hen) carries the mutation, because it is not linked to the sex. It is called an autosomal mutation, and as the mutant is recessive in transmission is thus a simple autosomal recessive mutation. One bird has the genotype of WW and the other is thus Ww (each letter representing the genes of the parent for that feature). In calculating the potential offspring from this pairing we must consider every possible permutation of the genes, for it is random chance which gene from the one parent will combine with one of the two genes of the other parent. We can calculate the results of this pairing very simply: WW x Ww = WW Ww WW Ww

The W of the first parent can combine with either the W or the w of the other parent. Likewise, the first parent's other W gene can do likewise. We have thus considered all theoretical expectations. Translated these will be: 50% homozygous normals (selfs), and 50% heterozygous normals split for white.

If two of these known white carriers were to be paired, the result would be as follows: Ww x Ww = WW Ww wW ww

Translated into phenotypes this would mean: 75% normals and 25% recessive whites. The whites are purebreeding (homozygous) and thus visual whites. The normals, however, comprise 25% purebreeding and 50% non-purebreeding (for their color), though all will look the same in appearance. Were you to have paired two normals of unknown ancestry, the fact that a single white bird should appear would tell you immediately that neither of the parents were pure for their color pattern—otherwise no white chick could have resulted.

However, our results are theoretical and it is possible that no white chicks would appear because of the random nature of the way eggs are fertilized by the sperms. The chance is 1 in 4 of obtaining whites. Only further matings using the same birds could attest, with any degree of certainty, the genotype of the parents. From this simple example it can be seen just how important it is to know the genotype of your birds if you wish to breed for given colors. It could save many wasted matings. If the ww whites are paired, you can see that the only offspring will be white.

Other examples of colors transmitted as simple recessives are opal, ino, and topaz in colored canaries. The Lizard variety is regarded as a recessive mutation, but it is not a simple recessive and its status is only partly understood at this time. Do note that where autosomal recessives are concerned, a bird *must* have both of the genes of a pair for that feature before it is visual.

DOMINANT MUTATIONS

The vast majority of mutations in animals

It is important to know the genetic background of your breeding pairs so that no time is wasted trying to achieve the desired results.

are of the recessive type, but there are always some dominant mutations. Examples in canaries include the crest, the so called "yellow" feather type (also known as the non-frosted or intensive), and the dominant white color. Only one of a pair of genes needs to be dominant in order for it to show itself visually, as was shown in the normal x normal/recessive white example.

When dominant

mutations are encountered, they may sometimes be associated with either prenatal fatality, or with some adverse effect in the individuals carrying them. As such, the heterozygous form is often the preferred, or obligatory state. In the Manx cat all examples are obligate heterozygotes (Mm), because the homozygous (MM) form of this mutation is fatal. In canaries the crested (CC) canary is a similar situation, the chicks die in the embryonic state or while immature. The recommended mating is therefore crest to non-crest as this will produce the following results: Cc x cc = Cc Cc cc cc, 50% crested (heterozygous) & 50% non-crested (homozygous).

If two crested birds are paired, the results will be: Cc x Cc = CC Cc cC cc, 25% non-viable homozygous crested, 50% crested (heterozygous), 25% non-crested (homozygous).

Given the value of what are called crest bred canaries, in studs in which the crest is a feature, it should be mentioned that the initiator theory advanced in budgerigars would suggest that the genes controlling the crest may not actually be dominant. They

Gloster Fancy pair. When breeding the Gloster fancy canary, a crested bird must always be paired with a non-crested.

may be incomplete dominants, and two pairs of genes may be involved, rather than a single major gene as has always been assumed. For practical purposes you can work on the assumption that the crest is a simple dominant.

Regarding feather type, this is not associated with a fatal situation, but rather with a general degeneracy of the feathers. The normal feather (called buff, frosted, or non-intensive) in the homozygous state is associated with feather lumps if continued buff to buff matings are practiced. If yellow to yellow (feather type not color) is practiced, this is associated with decline in feather density. The desired mating is therefore buff to yellow (yy x Yy) as this will produce 50% of each variety.

SEX LINKAGE

When a gene that is situated on one of the sex chromosomes mutates it is known as a sex linked mutation. In calculations, to work out expectations from such mutations, the sex of the bird must always be considered. All present sex linked mutations in canaries and other birds are of the recessive type.

You may recall that the Y chromosome of the sex cells is shorter than the X, and this has an important bearing on expectations. Being shorter, it does not contain the same number of loci as does the X. This means that any features, such as color, which may appear on the X chromosome, have no counterpart on the Y. It appears that the only genes on the Y chromosome are all to do with sexual features.This results in a recessive gene showing itself visibly when in single quantity.

The sex linked genes in canaries are agate, pastel, satinette, ivory, and cinnamon (brown). As the cinnamon color is available in all canary varieties, the others being features of colored canaries, we can use this as our example. We can commence by pairing a cinnamon cock with a normal hen. The cock will have the genotype of XcXc, while the hen will be XCY. Note that with each X chromosome we indicate the color

carried on this. There is no corresponding portion on the Y chromosome, so no color is possible on it.

XcXc x XCY = XcXC XcY XcXC XcY This translates as follows: 50% normal cocks/ cinnamon (visually normal but carrying cinnamon), 50% cinnamon hens.

A point worth remembering in respect to hens that show the sex linked color is that they can be regarded as being homozygous. They cannot be split for a sex linked color—they either display it, or they do not have it.

We can look at a second example involving cinnamon. Let us pair a normal cock, which is split for cinnamon, with a cinnamon hen. The cock's genotype will be XCXc, while the hen's will be XcY. A punnet square is very useful to work out calculations with two or more pairs of genes. The genes of the cock that can be passed on are placed along a horizontal line; the genes which the hen can pass on are shown in the vertical plane. The squares created are then simply filled in.

A final point of note that is not always appreciated by beginners is that the normal hens from this sex linked mating can never produce cinnamon offspring unless paired to either a cinnamon cock or one split for this. They are in no way carriers of the cinnamon gene, so the fact they were bred from a visual cinnamon, and one that was split for cinnamon, has no bearing on their own breeding potential for this factor.

EPISTASIS

A very important aspect to be discussed in this basic introduction to genetics is in respect of a gene's power to mask the presence of all other genes for a feature such as color. Such genes are said to be epistatic.

When breeding for fun it is not important to know the finer parts of genetics, however, the basics should be understood.

Normally, genes at a given locus will either   be seen or not seen based on their genotype, that is if they are recessive or dominant. However, it is possible for a gene at another locus to influence their appearance. Albinism, as seen in the recessive white, as well as dominant white, is such an example.

It must not be assumed that when a bird is all white, it no longer contains the genes for color. It does in fact have every single color gene, but these are prevented from developing color by the presence of the dominant gene for white, or by the homozygous state of the recessive white. These genes do not remove the color genes, they merely prevent them from forming color. This is easily shown if single factor dominant whites are paired. From such a mating there is a 1 in 4 chance of obtaining normal colored birds, and these will have no genes at all for the white factor. This shows that the parents must have passed color genes to the chicks even though they (the parents) were both pure white.

The simplest way that you can think of genes is perhaps in respect of colors. It is not known how many genes control this aspect of a bird, but let us use a hypothetical figure of 60, which means 30 pairs (thus 30 loci). These loci are never destroyed or missing (other than in aberrants), nor do they ever merge to create a sort of half-way result. At every single loci your bird has either the normal gene or one of its mutated forms. If your birds display only one known mutation, say the opal pattern to feathering, then they must cither be normal at every other loci, or have single recessive genes hidden.

Of course, a bird may be carrying a number of such recessive genes, which is why some breeders are perplexed when a mutants color or other feature suddenly appears in a chick. When it does, you know both of the parents must have carried this gene.

Most people find genetics a baffling subject, which it is. It really is worth persevering. You may need to read this chapter (and those in other books) many times before a given principle is understood. An explanation in one book may fail to deliver a point that may become apparent in another text, and vice versa.

The exhibition season runs from September through April, however, the training and work involved in getting a bird ready for the show is continuous.

Exhibiting Canaries

The exhibition side of the canary fancy is both fascinating and essential to the hobby. It is the means by which breeders can see how their breeding program is progressing. At a show their birds will be in competition with stock from all over the

This is a typical show cage. Note the pastel coloration of the back wall, and the all wire metal front.

country. Expert judges will give an opinion, via the awards, as to which are the best birds. The exhibition is thus the shop window of the canary fancy, as well as being an integral part of it and of its development.

The amount of show training a bird requires is determined by its variety.

All potential canary owners are recommended to visit at least one or two shows because at such events, most of the varieties will be on display. There will also be, more so at the larger shows, dealer booths selling items. Shows range from small, local club level events to the large national exhibitions at which all species of birds can be seen. Such exhibitions may span two or more days and are real spectacles.

THE SHOW BIRD

When you are at a show and

looking at a winning bird, it is not immediately apparent just how much work and time the owner has devoted to "staging" his or her winner. The standard of competition is so high these days that unless an exhibitor is truly dedicated, any hopes of wins, or even places, will be restricted to local events, not major ones. The show bird is the result of careful selection, rearing, and training.

Once a bird completes its first molt, training for exhibition begins.

The show bird must be capable of being confined for long periods in a small show cage, yet still look lively on its perch. It must be able to withstand the long hours of transportation, and then many hours with thousands of people walking by and staring at it. This requires not

Shows can be limited to one particular canary variety—as this Yorkshire exhibition. Judging is typically done in this style at a show.

only a bird of very steady temperament, but a very fit one. A competitive bird may be expected to be staged every other week, so stamina is yet another quality desired in a good canary. It must not only look good, but its color must be correct. The needs of a show bird also place great demands on its owner.

SHOW TRAINING

Training a potential exhibition canary will normally begin at the time it is to commence its first molt. At this stage it will have just been weaned onto seed and ready to be placed into a stock cage. A show cage is fitted to the stock cage door such that the young bird can hop in and out of this. As an inducement to do so, some favored food items can be placed into the show cage.

Once the youngster has no fear of the show cage it can be placed into one and left in this, initially, for no more than an hour at a time. The next stage in its training is that people are

encouraged to view it—wearing spectacles, hats and other items of clothing that the bird may never have seen before. It must also not be frightened at the

Gloster Fancy-corona. Most show birds are bathed by hand two days prior to a show to allow the birds to dry thoroughly and regain the natural sheen to their feathers.

Yellow ground frill canary. Exhibitors have special combs and brushes to ensure the feathers of the frill varieties lie in the proper direction.

sight of other canary colors it may not be familiar with—white for example. The diligent exhibitor will move the youngster's cage around the birdroom such that it is placed high and low on staging as may happen at the event. The objective is to create as many similar situations in training as the bird will meet once it arrives at the show venue.

Variegated red-factor. When training a show bird it is important to have a number of different people walk past the bird's cage to steady him for such an audience as at a show.

The reason for all this training is so that when the judge arrives to assess the bird it does not flutter into a corner where its better points cannot be seen. The judge will try to encourage such a bird onto its perch, but obviously there is a limit to the judges time. It is the exhibitor's duty to present a bird that is confident and up on its perch where it will show itself off to its best advantage. Many a somewhat inferior bird has won at a show essentially because it showed well, while a better bird failed because it was not as well trained.

SHOW PREPARATION

Apart from the actual training, a canary must be meticulously prepared for a show. The process is actually year 'round, but peaks in the weeks prior to a show. Color fed varieties must be watched so that their color is as even as possible, and not in excess of the desired shade. Non-color fed varieties should display no evidence of color feeding. Sometimes this may be done by accident when feeding a branded softfood that contains a coloring agent. The exhibitor must be highly attentive to all matters regarding nutrition.

The feathers must be kept in fine condition by baths and sprays. A week or so before a show, many exhibitors hand bathe their birds. The novice exhibitor is best advised to watch an expert do this. Such a novice can do no better than try to find a seasoned exhibitor who will take him or her "under their wing" and guide them into this side of the hobby.

If a breeder wishes to be a regular exhibitor, it is necessary to select two or three teams of birds so that each week one of the teams can be shown while the others are recouping from their last outing. It is unwise to attempt to over compete a bird.

SHOW CAGES

The show cages used by the canary varieties differ considerably in their designs and dimensions. There are about twelve different styles (some varieties do use the same

A few of the colorful awards received at a show. Most breeders enjoy seeing the results of their hard work recognized.

Unlike most livestock shows where the animal gets the status, it is the breeder who gets the status when showing birds.

design). Basically, these styles are those in which the cages are almost all wire, and those which are wooden with a wire front. Even those that look similar may differ in detail, so it is a case of the exhibitor obtaining the correct one for the variety being shown.

It is essential that canaries are displayed in a very clean cage, otherwise this could loose presentation points. Before each show the good exhibitor will touch up any paint that might have been chipped or scratched. The cages must not have any marks of identification on them—each is given an entry number when the birds are staged, and only the stewards and officials know which cage belongs to which exhibitor. This ensures total fairness of judging.

JUDGING

Canaries only compete with each other indirectly, because they are judged against an official standard of points for the variety. The bird with the highest score is thus the winner. In reviewing the various standards, that of the Border canary is unusual in that it is the only one that specifically gives the judge the latitude to credit birds of outstanding merit via the 10 points allocated to elegance.

In terms of judging philosophy, for all varieties other than the Border, one could say that the best bird was the one that lost the least points. Such a bird may not have any outstanding merit, but no particular faults either. Conversely, a bird which had some outstanding virtue would, in theory at least, gain no particular credit for this. The addition of elegance to the Border standard gives provision for an abstract virtue that takes in the whole bird. That is, the whole may be better than the sum of the individual parts, and is thus credited for this. Such a system compensates a bird that might loose some points on a part for part basis, such as the head, color, or wings, yet which has the overall virtue of being a most beautiful specimen. Judging philosophy is a fascinating area of discussion.

Clear yellow Scotch Fancy. The Scotch Fancy is trained to hold itself in its unusual posture on command only.

The actual judging procedure varies from country to country, but basically falls into one of two types. In the UK, Australia, and some other countries, the judging is done behind closed doors and before the public and exhibitors are allowed into the venue. Thus, when everyone is allowed into the venue the judging is complete for most awards, and the ribbons and cards are already in place for all to see.

In the USA and a few other countries the judging is done in front of the public. This adds much excitement. Some countries are experimenting with both systems, as each does have its merits.

CLASSES

At a show, the number of classes scheduled reflect the support the show has gained in past years. A national exhibition of canaries has classes for all popular varieties, with the rarer canaries being classed as Any Other Variety (AOV). The varieties are divided into cocks and hens and into the various color types. Singing canaries, such as Rollers, do not compete at "type" canary shows, but have their own exhibitions. This is to ensure they do not pick up any bad sounds from birds not in their league for song quality.

Winning birds from each class go forward to meet winners from other classes. Eventually, the best of that variety, and the best opposite sex, are nominated. These will then go on to meet other birds for the best in show, or best unflighted, best flighted, best current year bred bird, and so on, depending what other classes are scheduled for any cage or aviary bird (i.e. including budgerigars, parrots, foreign finches, and softbills).

Apart from prizes awarded by the society sponsoring the show, there will always be a number of "specials". These are donated by other societies or by companies. To win a special offered by a society you must be a paid up member of it, and have noted this fact on your entry. If you forget this, the prize could go to a bird that yours had already beaten! Specials range from the best canary bred by a junior exhibitor, to the best entry from a given locality—there are no limits to the possibilities.

BECOMING AN EXHIBITOR

If you have visited one or two bird shows and would like to become a participant, you are strongly advised to join the society that governs your particular variety. At their local club meetings the members will make you welcome. If you tell them you are a rank beginner, they will be only to pleased to explain all aspects of exhibition. They will no doubt even advise you as to the quality, thus chances of success, of your birds. Most clubs will also organize club transportation to exhibitions, a very useful service that saves you much time.

Clubs have regular lectures and slide shows, as well as their own local shows. Local shows are the events you should enter first, as the competition will be less fierce, and the whole event is much more informal. At these, the judges have more time to discuss your birds with you (after judging is completed) than

at the major exhibitions. If there are no clubs for your variety in your area, check if there is a general canary club. Failing this there will almost certainly be a foreign or domestic finch society, and this will invariably have a number of canary breeders in it.

Fife Fancy canary. Each variety of canary has its own standard show cage and way of being prepared for the show.

Canaries are relatively nervous birds, however, after some time they do calm down and begin to trust you.

The Pet Canary

Canaries make very attractive pet birds. If you have a cock that proves to be a talented songster you will gain even more pleasure from it. The Roller, American Singer, and Columbus are but three varieties

With its beautiful song, pleasant disposition, and endless shades of color, the canary can add a special charm to any household.

developed specifically to be very good singers. If you want a top quality bird of these varieties you are advised to seek out a reputable pet shop. This way you know for sure that it is from sound, quality stock trained to sing well. If you just want a pet canary that will also have a sweet voice, your pet shop should also have a number from which to choose.

THE PET BIRD'S CAGE
The type of cage you

Pet shops carry a multitude of toys for all types of birds. Canaries most appreciate a swing in their cage. Ask the clerk at your local pet shop to assist you in a selection of these and other fine toys. Photo courtesy of Hagen Products.

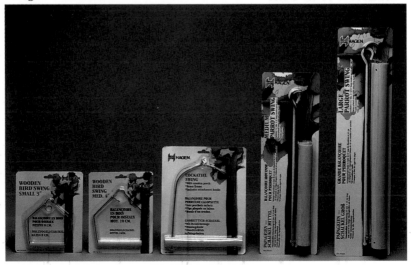

choose for your canary is an important consideration. There are no shortages of model styles, or colors, so it will be a case of how much you are prepared to spend. Do not be tempted to purchase a second hand cage. Its former occupant(s) may have died from a disease. Even after being well cleaned it is still possible for certain bacteria or fungi to survive, and be waiting for a new host on which to alight.

The main consideration of a cage is that it be as roomy as possible. Its shape is of some importance as far as the bird is concerned. Tall, round, ornate cages

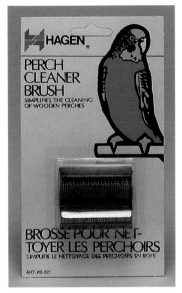

A clean perch is an important aspect of good hygiene. There are different styles available at pet shops everywhere. Photo courtesy of Hagen Products.

are of no value to any bird, especially a canary. They much prefer good length in which they can fly from one end to the other—or at least flutter. The size of the

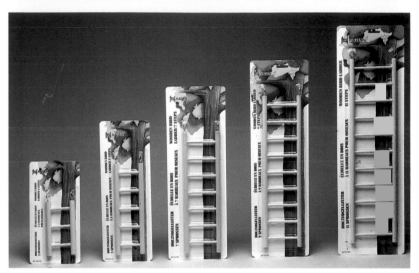

A ladder will assist your bird in getting around its cage. Your pet shop dealer will carry such items and be happy to assist you in your selection. Photo courtesy of Hagen Products.

cage becomes less important if you allow the bird freedom to fly around a room, which this author always recommends.

Other aspects of a cage are that it have no sharp pieces of metal protruding on which the bird might injure itself. It should also be easy to clean. It should not be cluttered with toys and other objects that might interfere with the bird's movement as it hops from one perch to another. If you plan to place the cage on a bird stand, consider the fact that many of these are not actually that good. The less costly stands will invariably topple over if knocked. Choose one that is heavily weighted or stands on four firm legs (rather than three). It is actually better to place the cage on a firm object such as a table or similar piece of furniture where there is no danger of it being knocked over.

CAGE LOCATION

The cage should be located such that it is protected from drafts.

There is nothing that a canary enjoys more than taking a bath. Bird baths can either be attached to the opening of a door, such as this Hagen Deluxe Bird Bath, or smaller tubs can be purchased from your pet shop that can be placed inside of the bird's cage.

Avoid placing it close to or opposite doors. It is likewise best not to place it too close to any form of heater because when this is switched off the result will be a sudden drop in temperature. Rapid temperature changes will quickly induce a chill in such a small bird. Although birds enjoy sunshine, they must always be able to retreat from this whenever they wish. With this in mind, you should ensure some shade is provided to the cage if subjected to direct sunlight. Always try to place the cage such that the bird is about at your head height. Birds feel very intimidated if you tower over them when you approach the cage. In any case, you do not want to be bending over every time you talk to the canary. If you wish to give your canary an extremely spacious home, an indoor flight is the answer. These can be purchased or made to fit into a suitable alcove or similar place.

BRINGING HOME YOUR CANARY

The best time to bring your canary home is as early in the day as possible. This allows it time to settle into its accommodation before nighttime. If you do not have a suitable small box in which to transport the bird, the pet shop will supply one. Make the journey home as quick as possible so the bird is not left in its transport box too long. On very long journeys the bird will be better off if placed into a cage with seed on the floor and the perches removed.

At the time of collection do not forget to obtain a supply of seed, together with canary sized grit, iodine blocks, cuttlefish bone, and any other supplementary items you may wish to purchase. Many pet bird owners also supply mirrors and bells to their pets.

HAND TAMING

To obtain the maximum enjoyment from your canary it will need to be hand tame. In order to be hand tame, it needs to overcome its fear of humans. Once this is achieved it will have no fear of flying to you and perching on your arm, shoulder, head, or finger. Such a bird will be easy for you to place into its cage when the need arises. In fact, a tame canary will often return to its cage without your help because it will regard this as its home, rather than a prison—which is how many non-free flying pets view their accommodation if they get the

Hand taming a canary requires a great deal of patience.

A canary cannot be tamed until it shows no fear of your hand when you place it in the cage.

opportunity to escape from it.

Hand taming is easy to achieve with a young bird, especially one straight from the nest. It can also be achieved with adults; it just takes longer for you to win their confidence. Commence the taming process by talking soothingly to the bird. Once it shows no fear of you approaching its cage, offer it tidbits through the cage bars. The next stage is to place your hand in the cage and take it out again. This should be repeated a number of times until the bird shows no particular fear of this.

Next, you can steadily move your index finger towards the bird and place it under its chest. It will either flutter away or hop onto your finger. This should be repeated many times until the bird is quite confident in perching on this. Ultimately, you can bring the canary to the opened cage door on your finger and it will fly around the room. With great patience you will arrive at the point where the bird will alight on your finger or hand. Eventually, you can win the bird's confidence to the degree that it will let you gently stroke it, but this does require very special and tender care. Such training is best done when you and the bird are alone in the room with no distractions at all.

FREE FLYING PRECAUTIONS

If your canary is allowed free flying periods, you must take care that nothing could harm it. The following are some of the potential dangers in a room:

1. Open widows and windows not covered with curtains.

Watching a bird take a bath is almost as enjoyable for you as it is for the bird. It will flutter in many different positions to ensure its entire body becomes wet.

2. Open chimneys. Always ensure that chimneys are fully enclosed with a protective guard. Such guards should also be fitted to any extractor or similar fans.

3. Guards must be fitted to any electrical bar heaters so the canary cannot flutter onto these.

4. Fish tanks. These should always be fitted with a cover glass and hood (which is better for the fish as well).

5. Ornaments. These may easily be knocked

Birds may be permitted to free fly around your house. You may even wish to place natural tree branches around for the bird to perch on if it so desires.

free flying. It is courting disaster, especially where cats are concerned.

You are further strongly advised to never allow your canary freedom in a kitchen. This holds so many potential dangers, such as gas or electric rings, boiling pans, and kettles.

GENERAL CARE

In order to help maintain the good health of the feathers

from a shelf by a bird, so for your own sake it would be wise to remove such a risk.

6. Dogs and Cats. It is unwise to have these pets in a room in which a small bird is

Opposite: Not all birds will hop into an enclosed bird bath. To coax a timid bird in, you can place a fresh spinach leaf or other favorite raw vegetable inside.

of your pet, a fine tepid water spray each week will be beneficial. This should be done early in the day so the bird has plenty of time in which to dry out. Even better would be to purchase a cage bath. These are clipped onto the cage, with the cage door in the open position. Your canary will really enjoy this.

Keep an eye on the length of the canary's toenails as sometimes these become overgrown, especially if the perches are too small. They are easily trimmed with sharp scissors, but be very careful not to cut near to the "quick" or blood vessel. This is easily seen in pink nails, but not as obvious in dark nails so do not trim off as much.

The pet canary invariably does not exercise as well as an aviary bird would, and may become obese unless you regulate its diet carefully. It will not need as many protein and fat seeds once it is an adult. Be very diligent in the matter of cleaning its cage every week as this will greatly reduce the risk of it becoming ill. Even though it may not be in direct contact with other birds, bacteria from these can be carried in the wind, or by you or other pets in the home.

No matter what color, posture, or song variety of canary you purchase, you will truly have an enjoyable time with your pet.

Good health is the result of a well balanced diet, good husbandry, and the knowledge of being able to recognize an illness when it arises.

Maintaining Health

In terms of animal husbandry, the clever owner is the one whose knowledge is based on how to avoid illness in his or her stock, rather than on how to treat it. Treating an illness requires a great deal of hands on experience with the problems and diseases, which hopefully you will never have to encounter—but your vet has! What you must be able to do is apply sound

Housing different varieties of birds together can only be done if the disposition of each is well known to the owner.

methods to your general care, know how to recognize an ailing canary, and know what actions you should take, short of actually attempting to treat the bird. In this chapter no specific treatments are cited; only general remedial recommendations are given.

GENERAL HYGIENE

The majority of problems and diseases encountered by birdkeepers can be avoided if more care is applied in two important areas. Specifically, general hygiene and nutrition. Other prime areas that are guaranteed to create problems are overcrowding, lack of quarantine, and delays in taking remedial actions once a problem has become apparent.

Disease is able to take a hold in any situation where there are a number of birds in close proximity to each other, and where the conditions are conducive for pathogens (disease causing organisms) to be able to multiply their numbers with little done to prevent this. Let us take a simple example. The perch a bird uses is a prime source of transmitting disease to other birds. This is because the pathogens can gain

Young canary chicks should be monitored carefully to ensure they are eating properly on their own. Very often chicks are taken away from their parents too soon and begin to loose weight.

access to other birds via their feet, feathers, and beak.

When at rest, the canary's feathers touch the perch, as

do its feet. When a bird has eaten, it will wipe its beak on the perch. It can thus both pass bacteria to the perch, and receive it from this. In spite of this fact many breeders use old perches that have long since lost the capacity to be well cleaned. Further, they are often allowed to become clogged with dried fecal matter and general dirt, thus becoming prime sites for bacterial colonization. The answer is to ensure perches are cleaned on a regular basis, more often if a greater number of birds use them. Destroy perches once it is obvious they are showing any signs of wear.

Feeder dishes must be scrupulously cleaned on a daily basis, as must all cage and birdroom floors. All seed husk sweepings should be removed as collected, not left in a bin or such until it is full. Cages themselves should be cleaned at least once every week.

When handling your canaries it is useful to wear disposable, surgical gloves, especially if the bird is ill. Always be sure to wash your hands after handling each bird. It is also advisable to wear a nylon overall in the birdroom. Parasites and other pathogens are not able to cling to this as they can to cotton and similar clothing.

Be sure that in the area immediately surrounding the birdroom there are no piles of rubbish, waste bins, garden trimmings, or other rotting vegetation. These are prime sources of fungal and parasitic activity.

Greens and vegetables should be removed after a few hours to ensure that they will not spoil.

Regarding nutrition, any vitamin or mineral that is lacking in the diet will usually result in weakening a bird's natural immune system. As such, it is more susceptible to disease. If the bird is receiving a well balanced diet, it should not lack any ingredients. It is then a case of ensuring the food supplied is fresh, and stored where it will remain so until eaten.

OVERCROWDING

When a breeder has a good season it

can happen that more birds are retained than there is really space for, resulting in overcrowding. Only you can determine how many birds you feel are enough for a given space. Having decided on this, be real sure you do not exceed the self imposed limit for any reason. It is far better to have a few healthy birds than lots of good birds that are always at great risk to an epidemic sweeping through them all. The more birds that huddle together on a perch, the greater the opportunity for pathogens to move easily from one to the other. Further, overcrowding usually results in greater squabbles, and therefore greater stress, which reduces a bird's ability to cope with even minor ailments.

LACK OF QUARANTINE

Lack of quarantine is an area a large number of breeders neglect, yet in so doing they place all of their stock at risk, and maybe years of hard work. Regardless of their source, all newly acquired birds should be quarantined as far away from the main stock as possible. If they should be incubating a disease,

Parisian Frill. Some of the rarer varieties are more delicate than the more commonly known ones. It is best to know each bird individually, from its eating habits to its fecal matter.

or if they are carrying a parasite, they can be treated before the problem is passed to any other birds. Apart from these aspects, you also have the opportunity

A bird's posture can tell you a lot about how it is feeling. Any change in its activity level or eating habits are also signs of ill health.

of studying the birds in isolation to see that they are feeding well on your selected foods before they are placed in your general bird community. You can also routinely treat them for parasites (external and internal) by using any of the proprietary treatments available from pet stores or your vet. The period of quarantine should be at least 10 days; up to 21 would not be amiss.

DELAY IN RESPONDING TO PROBLEMS

It can be very easy to look at a canary and think it doesn't look as good as normal. "I'll see how it looks tomorrow," is not an uncommon reaction. It can, however, be a fatal reaction for the bird and others in its company. A small bird, like a canary, can go downhill remarkably fast. If you are astute

enough to notice a canary is less than its normal self, you should follow through and immediately remove and isolate it, and any other birds in the same cage. If a bird has died suddenly, you must put yourself on red alert because all of your stock may be in danger.

RECOGNIZING ILL HEALTH

The non-healthy bird has been discussed earlier. All that needs to be added here is that once you have acquired an additional canary, you should spend enough time watching it to know its

If a diet that is varied enough is supplied to your bird, there really is no reason to supply added vitamins to its water or food.

character. Is it an especially active bird? Is it a greedy or dainty feeder? What tidbits does it really favor, and how often does it drink water? By observing these traits you will quickly notice any change in its behavior. Any change is a sign of stress or ill health. In some instances these may be the only clinical signs that will be displayed, and if you miss them the next stage may be the death of the bird. While a bird may enjoy a scratch now and then, it will not be doing this continuously, nor will it be sneezing or wheezing. These are signs of a problem, as are very liquid or different from normal colored droppings (droppings may of course change color if the food has changed recently). The more you study your birds the more their behavior will indicate to you the state of health they are in.

DIAGNOSING PROBLEMS

The main problem with diagnosing any bird disease, or a debilitating condition, is that the clinical signs for many of these are the same. Only microscopy and staining techniques can hope to be conclusive, and even these are not 100% accurate because there is still so much unknown about the diseases of small birds. This so, it can be very dangerous for a birdkeeper to attempt to diagnose a condition. A chill may be just that, but it might also be the first sign of a more sinister condition. You can assume that the more clinical signs of ill health you see in a bird, the greater the problem.

Your best course of action, once a bird appears unwell, is to isolate it, then make notes on your observations. To these you should consider if any other factors may be implicated in the problem:

1. Have any new birds been added to your stock of late?

2. Have any other birds been ill recently?

3. Have you found any dead wild birds, or other animals, near your aviary or birdroom?

4. Have you changed your seed

supplier recently?

5. Is there any chance the seed may have been fouled?

6. Have any other birdkeepers visited you recently? Have they had any problems you know of from talks with them?

7. Have you taken any birds to exhibitions recently, or attended such yourself?

8. Have you, or an immediate neighbor, used any pesticides near your aviary or birdroom?

Documenting this type of information has two benefits. First, it may give your veterinarian valuable clues to the problem. Secondly, it may help you to pinpoint the possible means by which the pathogens gained access to your birds. You will be much more on your guard against such access in the future.

Having recorded the case history, you then can take one of two courses. Either you can take the bird to your veterinarian for a physical examination, or you can commence preliminary treatment by placing the bird in a hospital cage. A physical examination will be the normal choice of the pet owner, the hospital cage of the breeder. If you do subject the bird to heat treatment, it would be very unwise to then take it hours, or a day, later to the vet. This would probably make matters worse, because of the fall in temperature in the bird's immediate environment. If the bird is a pet, transport it in its cage as this will no doubt contain some fecal matter that will be important to the vet for microscopy.

If you commence heat treatment in a hospital cage, it will be helpful to place some of the bird's fcccs in a plastic container so they can be examined by the vet. Your vet will then either attempt a diagnosis based on your notes and the results of fecal tests,

or will make a house call. Once the diagnosis is made, only then can a treatment be prescribed. Never attempt to diagnose and treat your own birds as this just might cost you all of your stock! The wrong treatment will merely make matters worse, and the wrong dosage is as bad as no dosage, or too much. It is very important that you treat your bird exactly in accordance with your vet's instructions. Do not cut the treatment short because the bird seems to be improving; this can be disastrous. It may enable surviving pathogens to build up immunity against the treatment. Should you have access to antibiotics without veterinary prescription, you would be very unwise to use them without consulting the vet. Further, if two treatments are used at the same time, or if one is used excessively, this can create great problems, even the death of your bird.

HOSPITAL CAGE TREATMENT

There is little doubt that heat treatment alone, in a hospital cage, has saved millions of birds over the years. Such a cage is therefore almost obligatory equipment for any birdkeeper who has a number of avians. Such a cage helps the bird in three basic ways. It reduces stress by the fact that the bird is in isolation and does not have to travel far for its food, nor maybe compete with other birds for it, as it might in a stock cage or aviary. It enables the bird to rest in solitude away from the hustle and bustle of the birdroom or aviary, and the heat reduces the bird's need to waste valuable energy in keeping warm.

You can purchase numerous models of commercial hospital

cages, or you can make your own. Purchasing models offers various options according to the price. Here we will consider the homemade unit. Begin with a single stock cage which has been well covered on the inner walls with a gloss paint. Alternatively, construct a box shaped cage using one of the coated timbers; these are easily wiped clean after each use. A suitable finch front should be fitted.

An ill bird will sit fluffed up to keep in its body heat.

You will need an infrared lamp as this will provide heat without bright light. The lamp may come with its own stand or with clamps to fix it onto the cage bars. One with a built in thermostat is the ideal, but a thermostat can be added to an existing lamp. The lamp is placed to one side of the cage so that the bird can move to a somewhat cooler spot if it desires. This method reduces stress that might occur in birds because they cannot move away from the heat source (i.e. in underfloor heated cages or those with glass fronts).

If no thermostat exists a thermometer is needed so you can monitor temperatures. The perches should be placed low down so no effort is needed to get on them, but they should be just high

An ill bird can and should recover very quickly from an illness. Just because a bird appears to have recovered from an illness, do not ignore it. Keep a watchful eye on the bird until all aspects appear well.

enough for the bird's tail to clear the floor. A shallow dish of water will provide the needed humidity. The temperature should be set between 29-32°C (85-90°F). If the bird seems distressed at the temperature selected, it should be reduced slightly.

TREATMENTS

Treatments for ailing canaries will usually come in the form of antibiotics given either via an oral tube, or by being added to the water. An oral tube is the better method as you can be sure of the dosage. When adding to water, the dosage is obviously dependent on how much the bird drinks. However, sometimes the act of handling and forcing a bird to take liquids can be counter productive, as it stresses or shocks the bird. Your vet will advise you of what foods to supply or withhold. If the medicine is in the drinking water it is best not to supply greenfoods or fruit, thus the bird is encouraged to drink.

Soaked seed, however, may be given for it is important that a small bird has some food intake otherwise it will rapidly fade. The medicines supplied will kill beneficial bacteria in the gut, as well as those causing the problem, so at this time extra vitamins will be needed to compensate for those not being synthesized by the bird. The vet will advise you on this matter.

Given the forgoing regarding heat and antibiotic treatment, a sick canary will either begin to make a recovery within 24-36 hours, or it will continue to deteriorate. In the latter case there is rarely much you or the vet can do. Should the bird die, an autopsy is recommended. It may enable the vet to determine the cause of death and thus suggest alternative treatment for others of your stock that may be at risk. It may happen that unless organs are actually damaged, the death is attributed to non-specific causes. This is because pathogens leave the bird shortly after it dies. In the event you cannot get the body to the vet immediately, it should be wrapped in cellophane paper, or placed into a plastic container and stored in the refrigerator, not in the freezer.

RECOVERY

Once a bird appears to be improving, you can slowly reduce the temperature in the cage. Upon complete recovery you can further reduce the temperature to that of the room. If the bird came from an aviary, it would be unwise to place it straight back until it has had a period indoors and is fully fit. If it is autumn or winter, it would be wise to retain it indoors until the spring, unless the problem proved to be only a minor condition that had rapidly been resolved with heat treatment alone.

PHYSICAL INJURIES

Should a bird break a leg or wing it is possible for your vet to immobilize and set this with a piece of strapping, a drinking straw, or even a matchstick. However, some birds will then persist in pecking at the support and may make matters worse. Your alternative, and one that is as successful as any, is to place the bird in a small cage with a single low perch. The fracture will knit together, though the limb may well be held in an abnormal position. This rarely bothers the bird, which soon learns to cope. A bird which has lost a leg can even learn to get about very well indeed.

EXTERNAL PARASITES

The usual body parasites of birds are red mites, lice, and fleas. Red mites and fleas will infest both the bird and its cage. Lice complete their life cycle on the host, as does the Northern mite of the tropics— so these are easier to eradicate. Apart from the direct damage these parasites do by the lesions they create when sucking the blood of their host, or in breaking down feather or beak tissue, they are also carriers of pathogens which gain access to the body via the wounds.

Parasitic infestation is usually a sign of poor hygiene in the cages and birdroom. The answer is thus to really have a good clean up, and to maintain this. Perches are best burned and the cages should be carefully cleaned in their corners, then repainted. At the same time the birds can be treated with a prescribed powder from your vet. Such treatment must be repeated until all the eggs of the parasites have had time to hatch and be killed. Bad lesions on birds should be wiped clean, and a suitable antiseptic applied to prevent secondary infection.

INTERNAL PARASITES

Parasites that invade the internal organs of canaries are many. Common examples may be mites that create respiratory problems, or worms that are found in the digestive system and other organs. Fungi are especially problematic because they can attack all organs, and are very difficult to eradicate. As with external parasites, these various organisms are found in poor living conditions and where food has been in constant supply for them. Only fecal and blood tests will confirm which organism is creating the problem (often a number are involved) so it is a case of again embarking on a big clean up drive, while seeking veterinary advice as to how the birds should be treated.

It is of course possible for illness to strike in even the very best kept birdrooms, but such an instance is quite rare, and usually the owner quickly prevents epidemics by his or her careful husbandry routines.

Lizard canary. The most distinctive feature of the Lizard is that of its plumage pattern. The pattern is that of overlapping scales as seen in reptiles, hence the name—Lizard canary.

Canary Varieties

In this chapter we will take a look at a number of the canary varieties that you should be able to obtain without undue problems. Some are highly popular and invariably for sale in pet shops, others are less frequently seen, so you might have to search a little to locate a breeder of them, or you can inquire to your pet shop owner if

Colored canaries. Left to right: Variegated intensive red, silver agate opal, gold agate opal, and silver brown. Unlike most canary varieties where type is the more important factor, it is the color that is of importance in the color canary.

they can be acquired. We can also take a glance at the rather rare varieties. These will be much more difficult to locate.

The descriptions are basic and intended to give you the features that are the essence of the variety. The many colored illustrations throughout this book will give you a much clearer idea of what these canaries look like. Some represent the

The Border canary is a well-rounded bird that appears dainty and elegant.

extremes of fashion in breeding for the unusual. The beginner is always recommended to begin with one of the more popular varieties. With these, you will find there are variety classes at most shows (rather than their having to compete as any other variety, AOV). You will also find there is a ready market for any surplus birds you have. Once you have become familiar with the canary fancy you will be better able to decide if the rarer breeds are for you. You will then have the contacts both to buy and sell the rarer breeds.

BORDER CANARY

History: The Border canary is the most

A well-rounded breast of a female Border helps in egg incubation.

popular of the canary varieties. It was named for the counties that form the border between England and Scotland. Its history goes back to about 1820, though the Border club itself was not formed until 1890, with the first model for the variety being announced a year later. An attempt was made to call this variety the Cumberland Fancy (an English county), but this caused quite a stir among the Scottish breeders of Dumfires, Roxburgh, and Selkirk. The formation of the Border club satisfied this bone of contention. It is not known from which variety the Border was developed, but the

Norwich must be pretty high on the list, based on references to early illustrations of both varieties.

Description: The Border should not exceed 14cm. (5.5in.) in length. It is a variety of nicely rounded curves, with a well developed chest. The head is rounded and there should be an obvious break where the neck joins the body. In a good stance the bird should display just a little of its thighs, and should

The Border canary is still the most popular canary variety available today.

have sufficient length of leg to give it a bouncy look, never squat, but never too "leggy." The feathers should impart a look of polished wax, but this is not so common today as in the past because of the use of buff feathering to give the illusion of good size.

You may hear reference to 4, 5, or 6 pointers among Border enthusiasts, and these relate to dark markings seen around the eye, on the wings, and on the tail. These are in contrast to the much more irregular patterning seen in the average variegated birds (ones with a mixture of dark feathers spread among those of yellow). The variety is seen in various colors, such as yellow, green, cinnamon, and white. It may be ticked or variegated, both of which refer to the amount of dark pigment appearing in the feathers. This variety is not color fed.

Comment: The Border is an extremely attractive variety that is one of a number that perhaps epitomize what the average person thinks a typical canary looks like. It is a highly popular show bird that has been bred to a very high standard of perfection. Potential exhibitors will find no lack of top competition.

The crest of the Gloster must radiate evenly from the center of the head so that the crest sits perfectly on the head.

GLOSTER CANARY

History: This delightful and dainty little variety is a relatively recent breed that was developed during the early 1920s. It is named for the county of Gloucestershire in England. Its originator was a Mrs. Rogerson, who had a great love for all diminutive things. The breed was helped considerably by a prominent canary breeder of his day, Mr. A.W. Smith, who also wrote the first small book on the variety. The Gloster is the result of crossings between small Border canaries and the crested Roller variety. From its first show appearance in 1925 the variety has steadily gained devotees throughout the world, and is always very well represented at bird exhibitions.

Description: The Gloster is seen in two forms, one being the crested, known as the corona, and the other being the plainhead, called a consort. When

The crest of the Gloster must neither be too large or too small. When viewed from the side it should cover half the eye, not all of it.

breeding this variety a corona is paired to a consort. This will produce 50% corona and 50% consort. The corona is thus a heterozygous bird, while the consort is homozygous. By such pairings the lethality of the double gene controlling the crest is avoided.

The feathers of the crest are most important. They should radiate like petals on a flower from the center of the skull, so that the crest sits perfectly on the head. The veins of the feathers should be black with green edging. However, clear crests are accepted, as are those termed grizzled which are flecked with black. The crest must be neither too large nor too small. When viewed from the side it should cover half the eye, not all of it. The back of the crest should flow evenly into the nape of the neck,

Gloster Fancy consort. The Gloster Fancy is a small, roundish, and compact bird that is lively and bold.

with no suggestion of a drop. The beak should be small and just visible. A large beak would ruin the balance of this variety where the impression must always be of a dainty bird.

Whereas the Border is a bird of rounded contours with an obvious neck separating the head from the body, this is not true of the Gloster. The chest is rounded, but the back is straight. The head blends gracefully into the body, so the neck is actually quite broad. The feathers of the wings should just meet on the rump. Those which overlap are too long, those which are too short will leave a gap, both being faults, not only in this variety, but also in all others.

The conformation of the consort's head is vital to the variety. Such a bird is every bit as valuable as that with a good crest. If the consort's head is not nicely balanced and round, it will result in offspring whose crest does not sit nicely on the head. As with all varieties, it is a case of viewing as many birds as possible — both pet and exhibition standard. You will then appreciate the differences in good and bad crests. The legs of the variety must be in keeping with the concept of small size. The desired state is that, when perched correctly, there is more than 1.25 cm. (½ in.) between the perch and the bird's underparts. The Gloster is available in numerous colors and patterns from clear yellows, through greens, blues, and cinnamons, to white. It is not a color fed variety.

Comments: If you are looking for a small cobby type of canary, the Gloster could be the answer. The corona is the one that will probably appeal to the pet owner because the crest gives it a special charm. The breeder, however,

should pay as much attention in the selection of the consorts as in the coronas.

FIFE FANCY

History: The Fife Fancy canary came into existence following the steady increase in size of the Border canary that became apparent after World War II. It is thus a miniature Border canary. The variety was named for the county of Fife in Scotland by an early pioneer, Walter Lumsden. It is one of

Opposite: The Fife Fancy is a small version of the Border canary. As the standard of the Border grew larger, breeders desired a daintier bird as once existed; thus the Fife Fancy.

the newer breeds, dating back only to 1952, when its image was conceived by five Border breeders in a pub in Kirkcaldy. It became well established during the late 1960s, and has steadily gained followers around the world.

Description: As already stated, the Fife is a miniature Border canary. As such, it should display nicely rounded contours. The quality of the feather is very important to the variety, as it is with any small canary. When perched, its body should be held at an angle of 60°. The length should not exceed 11.5cm. (4.5in.). This variety is not color fed.

Comment: This is a small and lively little bird that is a very reliable breeder. It has a sound disposition that makes it an ideal bird for the first time exhibitor, or as a cherished pet.

The Yorkshire is the largest variety of British origin type canaries. The Yorkshire is usually described as a guardsman or an aristocrat because of its erect stance.

YORKSHIRE CANARY

History: The Yorkshire canary is one of the oldest of the present day varieties, its history dates back to the early 19th century. It has always been a tall bird, but in former years it was much slimmer, as is evidenced by early photos and drawings of the desired type, and the old comment that it could pass through a wedding ring! As with all old varieties, its ancestry is not known for sure, but it is generally held that the Norwich and

Belgium varieties, as well as the Lancashire Coppy of its day, all had a hand in its creation. It is often referred to as the gentleman, or guardsman, of canaries on account of its very erect stance. The Yorkshire Canary Club was formed in 1894 and the model of the variety has passed through a number of changes, the present ideal being created in 1961.

Description: The Yorkshire is a very large canary, being about 17.2cm. (6.75in.) in length. The overall balance of the bird is more important than length, given that a bird will be of good size. In very loose terms the variety is best described as carrot shaped, which immediately enables you to distinguish it from the much more rounded type varieties so far discussed.

It is also a "leggy" bird.Its thighs are very evident when it stands on a perch at the desired 60° angle. The feathers are short and held tight against the body. The wings are long but should not cross where they meet the rump. The tail is of good length and should be straight, not drooped. The head should flow into the neck with no obvious pinch, the same being true of the line from the neck into the body. The chest and back lines are of gentle tapering curves down to the tail. A good example will display a similar shape when viewed either in profile, or from the front or back. The variety is color fed, and is seen in most popular colors.

Comment: This elegant canary is not as popular as in past years, though it still has a large following as an exhibition bird. It is one of the more costly varieties. Producing a

At one time, the feathers of the Norwich were so soft that they could not penetrate through the skin and caused cysts to form in the birds.

good show bird is an extremely difficult task, so it is a variety that offers considerable challenge. Some breeders foster out chicks because in some lines the

The Norwich should be housed in a somewhat larger cage than the average variety of canary due to its larger size.

parental ability is not good. It is always better if you breed from birds that are known to be good parents, because accepting quality at the cost of poor parental ability is a negative path to take in any form of livestock breeding. The Yorkshire is a most desirable canary and one which will appeal to the discerning fancier.

NORWICH CANARY
History: The Norwich canary is one of the oldest of all canary

breeds. It is thought to have been developed from canaries that were introduced by Flemish immigrants to the area of Norwich, in the county of Norfolk, England. If this is so, its history may go back to the late 17th century. It wasn't until the 19th century that the breed, like many of the old varieties, really became of age, for it was a period where interest in all canaries was very intense. Its original claim to fame was in relation to its color, but today its type is also very important.

Description: The Norwich is a cobby type bird which may attain 16cm. (6.25in.), so it is a relatively large and bulky bird as canaries go. Its well padded eyebrows and cheeks make the eyes appear very small and inconspicuous, a feature which distinguishes it from all other varieties. The chest is broad and full, the head large, and the forehead well developed. The neck is thick. The overall lines of the Norwich are rounded, so any tendency towards a flat skull or an overweight back are faults. The tail, however, should be straight and follow the lines of the bird, rather than project at a differing angle, a problem with a number of birds in this variety. Perched, the Norwich should be at an angle of 45°. The Norwich is a color fed variety, and is seen in a number of colors, the clears and variegated being the most popular.

A problem long associated with the Norwich is that of feather lumps. These have come about due to the practice of double buff feather breeding in order to create a more imposing bird. The recommended pairing is therefore buff to yellow (non-intensive to intensive). If birds develop feather lumps, they should not be used for breeding regardless of their qualities. This is the only realistic way in which this unfortunate problem can be eradicated over a number of years.

Comment: The Norwich is a most attractive canary if it displays good shape

Gold-cap Lizard canary. A good Lizard has a light colored cap (gold or silver) that extends from the bill over the whole head to the back; this is termmed clear capped.

The flights and tail feathers of the Lizard should be as black as possible if exhibition is intended.

and color. However, it is not the easiest bird for the beginner to take on in terms of its breeding. It is most important therefore that you seek out a dealer of good repute, rather than acquire stock about which you know little or nothing of.

LIZARD CANARY

History: The Lizard canary's ancestry has never been documented with any authority. It is known that spangled type canaries existed in the early part of the 18th century, and were possibly of French origin. Some of these may well have been the forerunners of the old London Fancy variety, which may in turn have been responsible for the Lizard. It may also be that the Lizard and the London Fancy were contemporaries derived from a common stock. Both were very popular during the 19th century, but fell into decline as other varieties gained recognition, and as canaries generally began to feel the effects of competition from budgerigars and popular foreign finches as the 20th century got underway.

Description: The most distinctive feature of the Lizard is that of its plumage pattern. This is the only variety of canary in which the pattern is the main (but not only) criteria of a quality bird. The pattern is that of overlapping scales as seen in reptiles, thus the name Lizard canary.

The cap is another important feature of this variety and it comes in two basic types, the non-capped and the capped. In the non-capped, the entire head is covered with spangles which, on the head, are like black flecks. The capped head is either clear, broken, over-capped, or bald. Clear is the desired state, meaning the head contains no dark pigment in the feathers (it is gold or silver). The cap should begin at the beak, pass over the eyes, and sweep 'round to the base of the skull. A broken cap is one in which there are areas of pigmented feathers; an over-capped is where the cap extends into the neck; a bald face is where clear feathers extend below to the eye. The baldface is a disqualifying fault in exhibition birds. The spangling of this

The Scotch Fancy is a breed that one should try to propagate after some experience is gained with the more common varieties.

variety is not evident until after the first molt.

The conformation (type) of the Lizard is not a major feature of the variety, but thc bird should be of a cobby type with good width of back to show off the spangling and the "rowings" of dark marks on the flanks and chest. The colors in the Lizard are gold or silver, and the variety can be color fed.

Comment: The Lizard is a most impressive variety, but not one which is able to maintain large numbers of followers. This is because it is very difficult to breed quality show birds, and because the exhibition life of the variety is usually limited to a single season. The reason for this is related to the fact that the spangles get larger and hazy as the bird matures, so such birds are not quite impressive against the younger specimens. On the credit side, the more limited gene pool within the variety means the beginner may well be able to obtain very good quality stock. Success may thus come more rapidly than might be the case with the very popular varieties, providing one works hard at meeting the stringent requirements of thc show standard.

SCOTCH FANCY

History: The Scotch Fancy, which in past years was known as the Glasgow Don, is thought to have been developed from the old Dutch canary crossed with the Belgian canary of its day. This probably happened during the early part of the 19th century. By the later part of the century the Scotch had become very popular, but decline then set in for various reasons. Firstly, canaries suffered from competition as mentioned under the Lizard. Also, it would seem that the Scotch and Belgian types became very similar — enough that one could exhibit them under the name of the other. This sort of situation always proves disastrous. One must add that fashions or tastes in what was desirable, also changed as the years rolled by. The result was that the Scotch Fancy almost disappeared, but retained a small band of dedicated followers. There is every possibility that it will experience a revival in the coming years.

Description: The feature of this variety is its stance, this being a curve rather like that of a quarter moon. It is a large canary, and should never be less than 17cm. (6.75in.). When moving between perches it should maintain its curved lines. Its build is graceful, with the small head being carried on a slender neck, this continuing into the chest and back which taper gradually to the vent. All standard colors—clear (yellow), variegated, and selfs are available. It is not a color fed variety.

Comment: If you are looking for something a little different, without going overboard on this, the Scotch Fancy might just be the variety for you. The quality of its feathers has improved in recent years—buff to yellow being recommended. You may have to search around to obtain good examples. Check that the parents are good feeders as this has been a problem in the variety.

BELGIAN FANCY

History: The Belgian is a very old breed that may date as far back as the late 18th century. It has been instrumental in the creation of numerous canary varieties. It was possibly derived from the old Dutch canary, but this is not known for sure. It became very popular during the 19th century, as did any animal that was unusual or rare. The 20th century saw a change in tastes, and the bizarre looking Belgian fell rapidly out of favor, and has never regained its former status.

Description: Ideally, this should be a large bird of at least 17cm. (6.75in.), but most do not meet this requirement. Its main feature is the fact that its head and neck should be held at an angle of 90° to the body, giving it a hunchbacked look. In this respect, broad, well formed shoulders are essential if it is to carry the body in the required stance. All popular colors are available. It is not color fed.

Comment: Not everyone's idea of a nice variety; many who

see them for the first time think they are deformed. The Belgian is a specialist's canary, so your problem in obtaining them is not only to locate a breeder, but to find one with good stock — not always easy in a variety such as this. Even so, the breed's future is possibly better than it was not so many years ago because there is a trend back towards the unusual. The show posture is inherent in most examples.

The Lancashire is a breed that was commonly used in the creation of other large canary varieties, such as the Yorkshire.

LANCASHIRE CANARY

History: This breed is the recreation of the old Lancashire Coppy which became extinct during World War II. It is named for a north western county of England. The original Lancashire Coppy was a very imposing bird, and thought to have been produced via old Dutch lines crossed with crested Norwich canaries. Although it influenced other varieties, it was never itself a highly popular canary — only among the cotton mill and other workers of Lancashire towns. The present day breed was created using Yorkshires crossed with any crested varietiy.

Description: Potentially, this is the largest of any canary variety, with a length of 22-23cm. (8.5-9in.). It is a bird of good build. For exhibition purposes it must be clear, with no variegation permitted other than that seen on the crest. As with all crested birds there are two forms, the crested, in this instance called a coppy, and a non-crested, called a plainhead. The one is paired to the other. Color feeding is not permitted. Variegated birds are needed to form part of the stud because these are required to retain size and quality which can suffer with continued clear to clear matings. This applies to all canaries.

Comment: Looking back, it is perhaps surprising that the Lancashire became extinct, because it is a very imposing bird. The variety certainly offers the newcomer the opportunity to commence with a variety still in the making. However, there are problems, because it is important that size be a priority, attention to the quality of the crest must not be sacrificed unduly. Being a large bird, it may be wise to have some foster birds on hand as large canaries are noted for being suspect parents.

COLUMBUS CANARY

History: The Columbus canary is named for the town of Columbus, Ohio, where it was developed during the 1930s. While well known to American fanciers, it is little known to enthusiasts outside of the USA, other than possibly by name. The varieties used in its creation were the Norwich and the crested Roller canary.

Description: Superficially, the beginner might mistake the Columbus for either a Crest or a Gloster. It is a bird of no more than 15cm. (6in.) in length. In build it is cobby, like a small Norwich. The crest should be neat and central to the head, but it does not extend over the eyes as in the Crest, it being more like that of the Gloster. Its contours are rounded. The Columbus is seen in many colors, though clear is the ideal. It is not a color fed variety.

Comment: This is a nice variety that has a sweet voice, a heritage of its Roller ancestry.

Being larger than a Gloster, and with a shorter crest than the Crest, it is a sort of intermediate variety. It has yet to gain international status partly due to the problems of exporting it to countries like England, and partly because of the obvious popularity of the Gloster, and to a lesser extent the Crest. It is deserving of more support in its homeland.

The nape of the Crest canary is short and stocky and its neck shows no indentation.

CREST

History: The mutation that is responsible for all crested canaries is known to have been in existence for well over two hundred years. Exactly when it first appeared is not known. Initially, it was merely a curious "extra" to the singing canaries, or Rollers, of the Hartz mountain area of Germany. During the 19th century crested canaries were paired with the Norwich to produce the crested or Turncrown Norwich. This became the king of the fancy, and remained so until the early years of this century. The Crest canary as a variety is thus the onward progression of the crested Norwich, but with all the attention

The feathers on the crest of a Crest canary are long and broad and come down over the bill and eyes. When vied from above, the crest should be circular and well filled in.

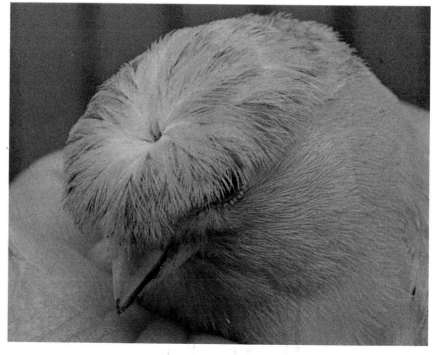

being focused on the crest.

Description: The Crest canary is seen in two forms, the crested and the plainhead. The crest of this variety is its main feature and should be as large as possible. Unlike the crest in other varieties, it obscures the eyes and extends beyond the beak. It must be perfectly symmetrical, radiating from a central spot, and it must sit perfectly on the head. Anything less than this is a fault to a greater or lesser degree. Type is not a major factor, but the variety will remind you of a Norwich. Color is not significant, though clear birds with dark crests were the ideal state in past years. The variety is not color fed.

Comment: The Crest canary is no longer seen in its former numbers, as other crested varieties have become more popular. To succeed in the variety you must place high priority on the feathers of the crest — as well as those of the body as the two are interdependent. The quality of the plainhead is, as in all crested birds, equally as important as the crested.

FRILLED CANARIES

History: As with most old canary varieties, the origins of the frilled canaries has been lost in antiquity. It is generally thought that the present day varieties, if tracked back in time, would converge on the old Dutch canary which existed in a frilled form. Presently, there are at least ten varieties of frilled canaries, these ranging from passably attractive to the rank grotesque — depending on your views of what constitutes beauty.

Description: The essence of all the varieties is the fact that the feathers of the body curl in various directions. You can also have a crested frill. Possibly the oldest of the existing varieties is the Northern Dutch Frill. This displays three areas of frilling. These are the mantle (back), craw (chest), and the fins (flanks). The

Northern Dutch Frill. Frilling of the Northern Dutch occurs in three basic areas; the mantle, jabot (breast), and flanks.

quality of the feathers and their shape is more important than the number of feathers, though obviously a well feathered bird is preferred to one with sparse feathering. In shape, the Dutch Frill is rather similar to the Belgian canary, though of less extreme type in the show stance. Color is not important and the variety is not color fed.

Most frilled varieties are large birds and the Parisian, at about 20.9cm. (8in.), is probably the largest. All of the frilled breeds display the influence of the Belgian, to a greater or lesser degree, some looking more like the Scotch Fancy, others having the obvious stance of the Belgian. The most bizarre frilled varieties are the Gibber Italicus and the Giboso Espanol, both of which

Much inbreeding is needed to retain the characteristics of the frilled varieties.

display sparse intensive feathering. Of the crested frills the best known are both Italian, the Padavon and the Fiorino (Florin).

Comment: From a management viewpoint, frilled varieties need careful attention because some are rather nervous, some have small clutch numbers, and most are not the best of parents. For these reasons it may be wise to have other varieties breeding at the same time in order to be able to foster out some of the eggs. It is unlikely the average newcomer will be attracted to the frilled canaries, which is possibly as well,

because they are better for being managed by a breeder with previous canary experience.

COLORED CANARIES

Unlike the situation in the canary varieties so far discussed, the color of the colored canaries is the all important factor, type accounting for but 10 of the possible 100 points in most standards. There are thus yellow, white, blue, and green colored canaries just as there are type canaries with these colors. It is the purity of color and the quality of the feather that distinguishes the color canary from all other varieties. It is the red-factor and

Canaries that are not fed coloring agents before the onset of their molt will result in spotty plumage coloring.

pastel colors that most newcomers tend to think of when colored canaries are under discussion.

History: The dominant and recessive white mutations, together with the brown (cinnamon), were established in type canaries as far back as the early 19th century. It was the arrival of the red-factor canaries in the post World War II era that really gave impetus to the "new colored canaries." This set in motion a totally new area of canary breeding — that purely for color. The red-factor was introduced into the canary by hybridization with the Black Hooded Red Siskin of South America. Initially, during the 1950s, results were not especially startling. Often the red-factor

The intensity of the red coloration of a Red-factor canary is such that it should not be too brassy nor orange. One must monitor, very carefully, the amount of color enhancer used in the bird's food.

canaries disappointed the first time viewer. Things changed dramatically with the allowance of color feeding and a whole range of beautiful red canaries appeared.

It might be thought that it was thus the color feeding that created the red, but this is not so. No amount of color feeding a canary lacking the red-factor gene will appear, and more importantly, molt out, as a red bird. Once the red-factor birds became established, mutations began to appear that greatly widened the scope of colored canary breeding. When these are combined with the red-factor and the basic ground color of a bird, the potential range of colors is enormous, and makes the breeding of color canaries one of the most exciting and complex areas of the canary fancy.

Description: The colored canary is a bird of about 12.7cm. (5in.) in length. Its type is quite distinctive when compared with any of the other "type" canaries, yet is variable within a given range. In profile the head is rounded, but not to the degree of the Border. Its back is very gently curved, while the chest shows a greater curve, but should not be cobby

Buff cinnamon Yorkshire canary. The erect stance of a Yorkshire is trained to birds from a very early age.

like the Gloster or Norwich. The tail is neither too long nor too short, and should look nicely balanced.

Colors: As mentioned, a number of mutations have occurred since the red-factors became a reality in the 1950s and these will alter the intensity of a color. For example, the ivory mutation dilutes the red to produce a pink-rose color, while it will change yellow to a pale lemon. The agate and isabel mutations are also diluting genes that differ in the way they act upon the melanin pigment in the feathers. These mutations, together with those for ino, opal, satinette, and topaz, have resulted in the vast array of colors seen in these canaries.

Comments: Colored canaries always fascinate the onlooker,

especially if they are an impressive color, such as intensive red or rose brown. They not only look good, but they have a sweet voice as well; making them desirable pets. From a breeder's viewpoint the colored canaries can be both fascinating and frustrating because colors do not always work out as one might hope. It certainly helps if you have a sound genetic knowledge, and it is very important to know the genotype of the birds you purchase. Attention to color feeding and any other factors (such as feather construction and light intensity) that may affect the ultimate color, are further subjects that are very important in the breeding of these birds.

Although it can be tempting to try and breed a number of color varieties, it is best to select just one or two of these and specialize, so you come to know the color really well. Progress is likely to be much better with such a policy.

SINGING CANARIES

It was the singing ability of canaries that first brought them into the homes of humans. As time went on, so the "type" canaries were developed. Although singing canaries have been

All male canaries have the ability to sing. There are certain varieties that have been trained to have a specific song such as the Roller, Waterslager, American Singer and Timbrados.

have a sweet song, but those of the singing varieties are an altogether different class — they are magnificent.

History: The first singing varieties were developed in Germany and Belgium. In Germany the birds were kept by peasants living in the Hartz mountain area. These birds are now known world wide as the Roller canary. In Belgium, in the area of St. Andreasburg, near Antwerp, miners developed the variety known as the Waterslager. The Hartz

around a lot longer than those bred for their appearance, it was not until the 19th century that breeders really began to study the song of the canary and thereafter to alter it to that which we know today. This is exemplified in the few recognized singing varieties. All canaries mountain canaries were sold throughout Europe. The British acquired large numbers of them during the later part of the 19th century, and firmly established them as a new extension of the canary fancy.

Some years later, in 1934, another variety was added to the songsters, this being the American Singer. This was developed by crossing Roller canaries with the Border canary (then a rather different bird than that seen today). Other singing canaries, such as the Irish Fancy canary (bred from the Roller),

Although this bird is all white in color it is not an albino because it has dark eyes. An albino bird is one which is totally lacking melanin, including the eyes.

and the Timbrados of Spain (which is a cross between wild canary species) have also been developed, but

The yellow coloration of most canary varieties is what most people believe to be typical.

are little known (the Irish variety now being developed as a type rather than a singing canary).

Of these breeds the Roller is without doubt the most popular, the others rarely being seen outside of their native countries. The Roller is judged totally on its singing ability in Great Britain, but in mainland Europe it can also be judged as a colored canary. The American Singer is judged on its appearance, condition, and song, of which song earns it 70 of the

100 available points.

Description: A Roller has no specific phenotype, and color is not important (only as mentioned in some European shows). The Waterslager is again a bird of variable appearance, though a standard has now been applied to it in Holland because it was being crossed with other canary varieties. The American Singer has a standard for appearance, but we need not discuss this as our present concern is in respect of singing. In all varieties it need only be said that singing canaries are very obviously canaries, and have not undergone any changes the way a number of type varieties have.

The Song: Each canary variety has its own song which it either learns or is taught. Its song is therefore not the natural one of the wild canary. The Roller and Waterslager have their own particular songs, while the American Singer learns any nice song — which may come from Rollers, Waterslagers or any other birds that possess a sweet voice. Canaries are very good mimics; so when they are young they are very impressionable. If they hear sweet notes they will copy them, if they hear a budgie chirping they will try to copy that, and this would obviously ruin their singing potential. Tapes and records can be purchased from pet shops to teach your canary different passages. Be sure there are no flaws or

North-Hollander Frill. The feathering of all frilled varieties is what makes them unique.

clicks on the tape that can be picked up by the student and incorporated into the passage.

The training of the Roller and the Waterslager is a highly skillful business and takes years to perfect. If you do not have an ear for music, there would be little chance of your producing quality singing Rollers. They are taught what are called rolls and tours. These are broken down into various sounds, called bell, gluck, hallow, bass, water, and other terms. They are sung in various registers — high, middle, and low, and must be delivered with quality of sound. Each canary has its own particular voice, just as any singer does. Some have high voices, others have a bass and so on.

The training of Rollers and other varieties begins as soon as they molt. They are placed in training cages with other youngsters to form a school. Sometimes a teacher is included; this being an adult that has a superb voice. This is not essential, however, because the song of the Roller, for example, is now inbred into it. The birds are placed in semi darkness and trained to sing when there is an increase in light. Once fully trained they are placed in cages with doors on them so they sing when these are opened—at competitions. The full training procedures are very complex and Roller breeders are extremely dedicated people who must learn much about the passages and the way they must be rendered.

Any birds that fail to meet the exciting standards required are quickly removed so they do not interfere with the training of the remaining birds. These failed students are sold as pet birds. Although they may be failures to the breeder, to you or I they have a magnificent voice and are thus desirable. A really outstanding Roller is a marvel and would have a very high value to a breeder — so it will never be available as a pet unless you were prepared to invest a large sum of cash, and maybe not even then.

The song of the Roller is based on the sound of bells and rippling water, whereas the Waterslager is based on the song of the Nightingale — both very different in their sound. Given the fact that these birds mimic other birds you will appreciate why Roller competitions are not held in conjunction with normal bird shows. The various chirps and whistles of other finches, plus the raucous voices of parrots, would have a very bad influence on these beautiful singers. The world of the singing canary is thus a totally separate entity to the general canary fancy, it is in many ways a world that few breeders really know much about, unless they are involved in it.

OTHER CANARY VARIETIES

There are a number of other canary varieties that have been developed, but which you are most unlikely ever to see unless you visit the country of their origin. Most will never become popular in countries such as Britain, the USA, Australia, or

Canada, but one or two may gain a respectable following if a few breeders were to import examples. Here we can only briefly mention them.

Hailing from Germany is the Munchener, a large variety with a smallish head and a gently curving back. It stands on long legs and is a very attractive canary. The Berner, named for the city of Berne in Switzerland, is another large variety. It may reach 17.8cm. (7in) in length. Again this is a small headed variety whose skull should be flat, rather than round. Its back and chest are nicely curved, but not so

The Gibber Italicus is a trilled variety with very sparse plumage. On the breast and the belly the feathers are so sparse that bald patches can be seen.

much that it appears cobby.

From Spain comes the Raza Espanol, a recent variety in terms of its world recognition (mid 1970), but much older as a known variety in its homeland. The Raza is a bird that must never reach 12.7cm. (5in.) in length; the smaller is the better. It has a flat head and should be a slim bird exhibiting no tendency towards being rounded. The same is not true of the Japanese Hoso, whose show stance is not so dissimilar to that of the Scotch Fancy, from whom, along with maybe the Belgium, it was developed. The Hoso is rarely seen outside of Japan, but has appeared at the World Show in Europe. It is accepted in many colors, including those classed in Europe and the USA as being typical of the colored canaries.

The foregoing are the varieties that may make it to your country, but there are always other canaries in the making. Most of them fail to gain recognition beyond their immediate locality because they are so similar to existing varieties. You may also see mule canaries, these being the results of those crossed with other finches to create a very attractive bird with the sweet song of the canary. Mule canaries are one of a kind; each having its special charm. They make delightful pets as well as exhibition birds, when classes are scheduled for them.

T.F.H. offers the most comprehensive selections of books dealing with pet birds. A selection of significant titles is presented here; they and the thousands of other animal books published by T.F.H. are available at the same place you bought this one,or write to us for a free catalog.

T.F.H. Publications
T.F.H. Plaza
Third & Union Avenues
Neptune, NJ 07753

THE WORLD OF
MACAWS

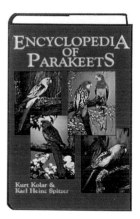

ENCYCLOPEDIA
OF
PARAKEETS

Kurt Kolar &
Karl Heinz Spitzer

A Beginner's Guide to
Parrots

PARROTS
A COMPLETE INTRODUCTION

Your First
PARROT

Martin Gabin

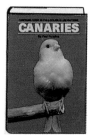

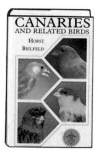

Index

Page numbers in **boldface** refer to illustrations.